IMPRESSIONS OF A FAMILY SCHOOL

100 YEARS OF ALLEYN COURT

JOHN WILCOX

To my sister Sally, and brothers Michael and Mark,
for patiently sharing in the aim that
Alleyn Court and its pupils should thrive.

First published in Great Britain 2005
by John Wilcox

ISBN 0-9549983-0-8

A catalogue record for this book is
available from the British Library

Design and typesetting by Stephen Morris, Liverpool and Bristol. 2005
smc@freeuk.com
Printed by MGA Printing, Southend-on-Sea, Essex
www.mgaprinting.co.uk

Lines from **Lent**, Michael Wilcox's 'Alleyn Court' play, first performed at the Lyric Studio, Hammersmith, in 1983. The BBC filmed version won many. awards.

Opening of the second movement of Elgar's Violin Concerto, played by Menuhin with Sir Edward Elgar conducting.

Paul: (checking and loading the school starting pistol) Last term we set up our own telephone service between the dorms. It was Abrahams who had the idea. He brought two sets of headphones back from Assam, where his father works. That's in India! He got some very thin copper wire... it was just a single strand... and we laid it under the lino when matron wasn't about. I don't know how it works, but when you link up the headphones at each end of the wire, you can speak into them like telephones, and you can hear what's being said! It's incredible! You can warn the others when Matey's on the prowl. The first message we got was 'HODGE HAS BEEN SICK!' There's a boy called Hodge and he was sick right at the end of Journey Into Space... all over his sheets. Matron was furious. She thinks Jet Morgan is terrible. We might not be allowed to hear it next term.

Harry Mortimer playing the third movement of Haydn's Trumpet Concerto.

Paul: Buffalo Bill was one of the best films I've ever seen. You saw his whole life, from when he was a boy like me, until he was practically dead. I liked it before he was famous. At the end, he had a circus, and you knew what an exciting man he had been. But the people didn't really care, and when he was old, with a white beard, he appeared in the circus ring for the last time. And he took off his hat to the crowd and the spotlights went off him one by one. And when the lights went back on again, he wasn't there, and you knew that was the end of him and he was going to die. That bit made me cry. Matey thought it was good too. He always gives me treats in the holidays.

Theodore Robert Wilcox

Foreword

The origins of Alleyn Court are treated in both the opening and closing sections of this book.

In 1910, the date of the first *A.C. Magazine*, Theodore Robert Wilcox wrote a piece reproduced here describing how he and his wife Ruth came to found the school in Westcliff-on-Sea. The final piece, *The History Lesson*, explores imaginatively the Lewis Carroll/Dodgson connection and the kindness that made possible the foundation of Alleyn Court and all that has followed.

Theodore Robert Wilcox was one of three children born to William and Fanny, both his father and paternal grandfather working for Customs and Excise. In spite of the death of his father when he was only eight years old Theo won a scholarship to the King's School, Canterbury and went on to read Classics at Selwyn College, Cambridge. Subsequently, for 12 years, he taught at Dulwich College Preparatory School, (hence Alleyn of course), marrying Ruth Mahon in July 1904 and together starting their own appropriately named school two months later.

I hope my grandparents are somehow able to appreciate their school's centenary as their successors continue the work they started.

Theodore as an undergraduate at Selwyn

John Wilcox, February 2005.

It has been suggested that a brief account of the origin and growth of the School should not be without interest to our readers, and I am afraid that from the very nature of the case the only person who can write such an article is the Headmaster. I therefore tend my apologies in advance, should my readers find the account tedious or the first personal pronoun a little too obtrusive. A little over six years ago I had never heard of Westcliff-on-Sea, and had only the haziest notion of the whereabouts of Southend, terrible ignorance on the part of a schoolmaster, but alas! the truth. Then in February, 1904, at the suggestion of a friend and on the strength of a glowing advertisement of Westcliff which I happened upon in a railway guide, I took the journey down and explored.

The result was that in August of the same year I found myself installed in what was at that time No. 3 Imperial Avenue, and putting up a brass plate on my gate I waited for the boys to flock in. Is it possible for four boys to ever flock, I wonder? At any rate that was the number with which the School started on the

Donald Williams

20th September, 1904, and perhaps the names should be recorded. They were D. Beven, R.B. Jackson, C.K. Jackson, D.M. Williams.

What a time we did have that first term! How we revelled in classics, mathematics, and all the other inflammatory branches of learning. What games of football we played! Sometimes we opposed an imaginary foe, and the five forwards would sweep down the field quite in the style of the Corinthians, and would never fail to finish up by putting the ball through the goal. Sometimes the match was Masters v. Boys, the latter generally winning owing to the retirement of

Ruth Wilcox

Masters from sheer exhaustion.

In January, 1905, we were joined by GRM Pakenham, but shortly after the term began, measles, that horrid type which is made in Germany, attacked us with such ferocity that more than half the School, three-fifths to be quite accurate, were laid low. The remaining two-fifths were ordered by the doctor to live in the open air, and his instructions were implicitly obeyed. Work was conspicuous by its absence, and the term passed very pleasantly, so the boys said. In September, 1905, much to my own relief, and still more so, I am sure, to that of the boys, who now numbered eight, we were joined by Mr Roach. At the end of the second year of the School's existence, that is in 1906, there were 12 boys, and then came a more advance, for at the beginning of the summer term of 1907, the numbers had increased to 25, while the staff, by the arrival of Mr Hilditch, now numbered three. At last there were enough boys for a full game of cricket, and we were bold enough that term to make a journey to Dulwich and play the Preparatory School, where I had spent so many happy years as an assistant master. We paid the penalty for our daring by suffering a severe defeat, but our opponents had over 200 boys from which to choose their eleven, so we may say that though beaten, we were not disgraced. In March of that year we gained our first success at the Public Schools, Allen being elected to an open Scholarship at Uppingham. May there be many more at Alleyn Court to follow his good example. In this year we moved from No. 3 into our new buildings, and I was also fortunate enough to secure the present playing field for the School. The year 1907 was certainly an eventful one in the School's history.

At the beginning of 1908 Mr Roach, whose help had been most invaluable, left us to take up work in London, and his place was taken by Mr Hammerton, who remained nearly two years. In spite of the time now having arrived when boys were leaving each term for Public Schools,we managed to keep up our numbers and last summer term there were 29 boys in the School. Another success was gained that term, Blagrove winning the first Scholarship at Dover College. It was quite appropriate that his name should begin with B. Are we going straight through the alphabet, I wonder?

We have now arrived at such recent times that this article must come to an end.

Theodore Robert Wilcox

Schools News *AC Magazine 1910*

Boys should remember that gardening must not be allowed to interfere with Cricket or other School games, but it is to be hoped that in their spare time they may find opportunities to attend to their garden, so that there may be as good a show as possible at the end of June.

Advice to Young Cricketers *AC Magazine Summer 1910*

The willow wield with all your might,
All unstraight balls be sure to smite;
Balls to the off past Point cut clean,
But keep them down upon the green
Or you'll be caught by Point or Cover,
And then your innings will be over.
Each straight ball play with upright bat,
Be very careful as to that.
All leg-balls to the boundry lift,
To hit them, though, you must be swift.
Ne'er use bad language on the ground,
E'en though the umpire be unsound,
And gives you out when you are not,
Accept his view, though it is rot.
Play always fair, in gen'rous strife,
Thus play the game, throughout your life.

WHC Mahon [Ruth Wilcox's father]

A Paper Chase *AC Magazine Christmas 1910*

An exciting Paper Chase took place at the beginning of the term.

The hares, Mr Hilditch and Smith I., were given ten minutes start, and, as all properly conducted hares ought to do, ran a big circle with Eastwood Church as the furthest point.

One of the hares went lame, and the hounds, running from scent to view, caught him, but kindly refrained from demolishing him, and he lives to run another day. The other hare reached home safely, but that good hound Clayton I. was close on his heels, and was unlucky in not securing blood. The pack on this occasion was reinforced by Miss B. Gregson, who ran brilliantly from start to finish.

The prizes given by Mrs Wilcox for tidiness and good behaviour in the Dormitories were won by Tremayne and Rankin.

Pansy *AC Magazine Easter 1911*

Some excitement was caused last term by the arrival of Pansy, the School pony. She took to football like a duck to water, and had a good chance of getting her colours when her methods suddenly became rather violent, and she is now fenced in and plays the part of spectator.

Armour-Plate Steel *AC Magazine 1911*

New Armour-Plate Steel Messrs. Krupp are stated to have produced, at Essen, a new nickel-tungsten steel, which has a resistance 11 per cent greater than that of the usual nickel-chrome combination. It is now asserted that a still further improvement has been made by another firm. The company is believed to have incorporated a type of alloy-partinum composed of aluminium and tungsten in a special steel, thus producing a plate which is lighter and tougher than ever the nickel-tungsten plate. This discovery is said to explain the activity displayed, in Cornwall, by Germany buyers of wolframite from which tungsten is obtained.

HMI

Editorial *AC Magazine Summer Term 1914*

What tremendous events have taken place since our last number was published. The boys had scarcely returned home for the Summer holidays when the storm clouds, which had been gathering during the last days of the term, burst in fury, and England was plunged into the mightiest and most terrible conflict that the world's history has known.

Editorial *AC Magazine Summer Term 1915*

The Summer Term was full of interest, not to say excitement.The two air raids are fresh in every one s memory, and no description of them is needed in these pages. Our special interest is the second, which took place on May 26th, consisted in the fact that three incendiary bombs were dropped in the cricket field; one missed the 1st XI pitch by yards, another the 2nd XI pitch by feet, and the third the fielding lawn by inches.We thank the Germans for the consideration they shewed! In spite of their kindness, however, it was thought prudent to move the boarders to sleeping quarters in the country for the rest of the term.We accordingly spent our nights at a delightful rectory six miles away, and our experience there, coupled with the interest of the daily drives certainly added, in the boys opinion at all events, to the pleasures of the term.

In Memoriam *AC Magazine 1916*

In Memoriam
Donald Matthieu Williams
Killed in Action in Mesopotamia, April, 1916

Donald Williams entered the School in September, 1904. Although there were three others with him when Alleyn Court started its career, he was the first boy to be definitely entered, and so for a short time he himself composed the School. And now it seems to come to us almost in the nature of a special message that he should be the first to fall, and thus be the one to remind us that this School, like all other schools, must pay its toll in the Great War.

He was a popular boy at Alleyn Court, and his bright little face and curly hair will remain long in the memory of those who were with him at that time. He subsequently proceeded to Lancing College, and when the war broke out, joined the famous Artists Corps. This led to a commission in the Royal Warwickshire Regt..

Editorial *AC Magazine January 1918*

The School has had something in the nature of a great adventure since our last number was published. During the first part of the summer holidays Westcliff and the neighbourhood was the scene of a nasty daylight raid, one bomb falling near enough to Alleyn Court to break several windows. This was followed a few weeks later by the first moonlight raid on London, and it at once became evident that the school must either move into safer quarters or continue to carry on at Westcliff with greatly diminished numbers and the prospect sooner or later of having to put the shutters up till the end of the war. To be brief, it was decided to move, and here we are at Englefield Green, installed in a large, comfortable house with lovely grounds and views.

From a school of 85 in the Summer Term we are reduced now to about 40; but they are all boarders, and our grateful thanks are due to several parents of day boys who by letting their sons become boarders are helping to keep the School together in these terribly difficult times.

Fragment of an original report of the visit of Princess Mary to Alleyn Court Preparatory School not from the Daily Telegraph following the air raids.

The flags were floating upon the breeze
in harmonious negligée.
A few had entangled themselves in the trees,
in the customary way.

On the cricket field's smoothly shaven lawn
so verdant across the way
was the little goat with the gilded horn,
and the pessimistic bray.

And Peter, the noble warrior true.
The hound that none can match,

decked in sulphur ointment and ribbon of blue
gave a loyal and fervent scratch.

And provision of hospitality note
surpassing the wildest dreams!
A dugout yawned with its cavernous threat
as a shelter from Hun machines!

And since confinement might irksome prove
Mrs Ramsey waited below.
And guarded that wondrous treasure trove
The Nicholson's Curaçoa!

But alas! for the passing of things mundane
when the Princess had motored on
Mrs Ramsey did still her post maintain
but the curaçoa was gone!

But I think you ll agree that the fairest sight
in all that dazzling scene
was the boys arranged in flannels white
with occasional mottles of green.

With hands and faces carefully washed
and his team arranged just so
the XI wore pretty white caps above
and bright pink socks below.

With pride and anxiety both possessed,
unhinged, though, with craven fear,
the Head stood ready with swelling breast
to lead the resonant cheer.

To Mrs Wilcox,
Fair arbiter of so many Destinies,
This fragment is respectfully dedicated
without permission by the author.

Visit of Captain Gordon Campbell VC DSO RN *AC Magazine October 1920*

When the Lords of the Admiralty, some time during 1915, sent for Lieutenant Campbell and asked him to embark on an enterprise which could not be exactly described as a very safe one, that young officer accepted with alacrity and proceeded to make his preparations with a secrecy which was positively irritating, his own mother knowing nothing except that he was growing a beard! In due course a German submarine was sent to the bottom of the ocean to stay there for ever and ever, while Lieut. Campbell had a pleasant little visit to Buckingham Palace and left with VC after his name. The whole world knows now of his exploits and the way in which he diddled the Germans, but to hear the story from his own lips was an experience and a privilege granted to few, for your naval man is the very embodiment of deeds not words, and it is as easy to get him to risk his life in some daring adventure as it is difficult to get him to talk about it afterwards.

However, Mr Wilcox still happily retained his authority over his former pupil so down he had to come to Westcliff and give the boys a yarn. The secret preparations and rehearsals, the departure in search of the prey, the find and manoeuvring for position, the sudden unmasking of the guns and the kill, these were all vividly described, and it is to be feared that there was not much sympathy to be detected in the faces of the boys when they were told that the first shell decapitated the captain of the German submarine as he was half-way out of the conning-tower. This was not known at the time but was told afterwards to Captain Campbell by one or two prisoners who were rescued. The body had toppled down below into the submarine and the feelings of the crew on seeing their officer return into their midst minus his head can be better imagined than described. Subsequently, owing to the suspicion and wariness of the German, it became necessary to be torpedoed first and then to put off what is known as a panic party, and the account of these proceedings was received by the audience with mixed feelings with intense admiration for the heroism of the men who practically asked to be torpedoed and afterwards shelled and yet had to wait patiently till they were in a position to reveal their true character and deal with the submarine; and with amusement at the realistic acting of the panic party who played their parts like professional actors. Not the least interesting part of the lecture was the life of the captain and his crew when lying at an English port and getting ready for their hazardous adventure. The deception had to be kept up even at home, and Captain Campbell, in his disguise as captain of an old tramp, had to hob-nob and, as he expressed it, spit about with his men during the day. It was only at night when they were below deck and free from prying eyes and curious ears that discipline reasserted itself and the disreputable old skipper became the smart naval officer once more.

Long life to him and his heroic crew!

Up Jenkins   *AC Magazine May 1921*

On the last Saturday of the term Exham and Mahon entertained Mr and Mrs Wilcox and the staff and nearly twenty boys at a most delightful supper party. Colonel and Mrs Exham were unfortunately prevented from coming, but Mr and Mrs Mahon were there and also Mr and Mrs Ramsey. After a most sumptuous repast we all sat down at one big table and played Up Jenkins, followed by a game in which a Ping-Pong ball was blown by one side of the table against the other. This caused an enormous amount of amusement and noise, and some of the players developed most colossal powers of blowing. As the evening wore on so did the noise increase until at last it was feared that our neighbours or the police might intervene, so we unwillingly broke up after tendering many thanks to our kind hosts.

We congratulate one of our old boys, H.M.C. Ionides, on winning the Sailing Race open to the whole of the Battle Cruiser Squadron. He is the youngest officer who has ever won the race and his crew consisted entirely of Midshipmen. Rear-Admiral Sir Roger Keyes especially congratulated him and handed to him a most handsome silver bowl presented by himself.

Williams House   *AC Magazine October 21 1921*

Talking of houses, we have decided to add a fourth called Williams House, in memory of Donald Williams, who was the first boy to come to Alleyn Court and the first to fall in the Great War. The house being, so to speak, in its infancy is not at present able to compete with the other three, but in a year or so we hope to see it holding its own.

A mock funeral   *AC Magazine May 1922*

Our Cambridge correspondent writes:-

J.W. Boddy (Emmanuel) plays golf of a kind but still vainly pursues a handicap. He is known to do a little work occasionally!

H. Mallinson (Caius) is a budding physician. How long he will continue to bud we do not know. He recently played a prominent part as chief mourner at the Mock Funeral for the Women's Degree up here. We observed him leaning out of the carriage window, his handsome countenance covered with flour and furrowed with tears.

F. Hawkes (Sydney Sussex) represented his college on several occasions in rowing; he represents his college in most spheres, where he thinks his college will adequately represent him. Our correspondent might have added that he speaks at the Union and contibutes poetry to the Cambridge Review and other papers.

H. Sellors was awarded a Cornwallis Exhibition at Oriel College, Oxford, last Autumn and we send him our hearty congratulations. He has got through all the Preliminaries in the Medical Exam, and spends his leisure time in hockey, footer and cricket.

Lectures and Cinematograph *AC Magazine 1926*

The arrangements for the Michaelmas Term are as follows:-

Friday, October 15th, at 6 pm
Films
(a) The Story of Peter the Raven.
(b) Betty's Day at the Zoo.
(c) My Father (incident in the life of President Lincoln).
(d) The King of Sports (Sword-Fishing in New Zealand).
(e) Tom Mix Comedy.

Friday, November 5th, at 6 pm
Films
(a) Studies in Animal Motion.
(b) Getting a new angle.
(c) White Fleece (Sheep Raising in New Zealand).
(d) The Lost Lie (Juvenile Drama).
(e) Felix the Cat.

Saturday, November 20th, at 6 pm
Lecture
My African Wanderings, by Mr J. Granville Squiers, F.R.G.S.

Saturday, December 4th, at 6 pm
Lecture
The Wonders of Flying, by Mr Oliver E. Simmonds, M.A.

Thursday, December 16th, at 6 pm
Not arranged yet, but it is hoped to get Zeebrugge.

Cambridge Letter *AC Magazine 1927*

Dear School,

There are now eight complete specimens of Alleyn Court culture in this famous and ancient seat of learning, and we are thinking of forming an Old Alleyn Courtian Society.

N.G.Wykes, now in his second year, is quite one of the leading lights of Queen's College. Last year he played cricket with great success, and we are all eagerly awaiting what the present season may bring forth.

J.W. Marsh is to be seen again after a term's successful seclusion among his books. Every day he roars down Jesus Lane with great velocity on a motor-bike in order to be in time to pull a lusty blade for Downing on the river.

We met P. Spagnoletti of Trinity recently at the sign of the Ram. No need, dear reader, to be alarmed at the sound of this, this is not the name of a low tavern, but of one of the most distinguished lecturers in Cambridge, Spagnoletti now keeps in the wilds of Chesterton, and is rarely to be seen in the domains of ordinary mortals except when pedalling vigorously to or from a lecture.We hope his tennis is as effective as his push-cycling, at which sport we learn that his bag for one day recently was two pedestrians and one policeman.

J.C. Ewing also graces Downing College, but is not very often to be seen about. We understand that he is very devoted to his books, though he is occasionally observed also to take air and exercise on the river.

We fear J.D. Neil of Pembroke is becoming a very military individual; not content, like the rest of us, to leave such things as the O.T.C. behind him at School, he has joined the Artillery, and is often heard to wish that he had started learning to ride a horse at Alleyn Court: his falls are hard and frequent. He also adorns the river, and one day last November was observed to take a bathe fully dressed; but this was scarcely intentional we think.

Trinity gleans two further Old Boys from Alleyn Court in A. Andrew and N. S. Fraser. Andrew is still very studiously applying himself to History, and we hear that he can ably conduct a very abstruse argument over the teacup. He and Fraser both manage to find time for golf, and also played hockey with notable success in the Winter.

Lastly we have one representative at Clare, in F.G. Hinks. For two terms he has been coxing one of the Clare eights, but he has put on weight so rapidly lately that for that or some other reason he is not seen on this river this term. Some explain the fact by saying he is working too hard for his medical exams to spare the time, but at any rate, he finds time, so he says, for an occasional game of tennis.

We hope that you will continue to add regularly to our number, and wish you the best of luck for the coming season.

Yours sincerely,

O.A.C., Cantab.

The Tie *AC Magazine 1928*

A letter from the Headmaster

My dear Old Boys

At last I am able to write to you; and to settle this matter.

Two of you,who were at the same public school, wrote to me some months ago, and asked if there could not be an Old Boys tie and made suggestions about it. I was very much taken with the idea, but it was a case of easier said than done. I had to get the right shade of grey which is the predominant colour here, and on that had to have the School Colours which, as you know, are Leander or cerise. I also had to make certain that whatever I chose could not possibly be mistaken for any well-known club, or regimental or public school tie. However, after many experiments, I have at last chosen a pattern and the tie is now being put in hand. Here are the necessary details. Write to or call upon George Lewin & Co. Ltd., 8 Crooked Lane Monument, EC3, satisfy him, by giving your name and address, that you are an old Alleyn Court boy and he will supply you with it.

The prices are 3/6. 5/-, 7/6 and 10/-; but Lewin himself recommends the 5/- tie. If you have any difficulty about it, write to or come and see me. I hope always to keep a small stock myself.

Now, I have nothing more to say, except to express a hope that, amid all the other colours which you are entitled to wear, you will not forget to wear this tie sometimes; it will get known by degrees down here, and in the neighbourhood, and if you live further afield, either in this country or abroad; two of you may meet wearing this tie, and it will be a sign that you were once at the same School;and will,I trust,act as a bond of sympathy between you.

I remain your most sincere friend,

T. R. Wilcox.

Death of the poultry AC *Magazine 1929*

Alas! the Alleyn Court poultry have come to an untimely end.

Early one Sunday morning towards the end of last term, an Alsatian hound, with a mongrel companion, waged such a ruthless war that only one chicken was left alive. The battle-field was really an awful sight; and the worst of it is that the combined efforts of all those at Alleyn Court, our next-door neighbours, the tradesmen, the police, and others too numerous to mention, have been unable to track to their homes the perpetrators of this dastardly outrage. The result of this tale of woe is there will be no more poultry at Alleyn Court.

Prix de Rome AC *Magazine 1929*

Most hearty congratulations from the whole School to R.J. Finny, who has won that great scholarship for painting called The Prix de Rome. The following appeared in the *Southend Standard* at the time:-

> *The most coveted Art Scholarship, The Prix de Rome has been won this year by Mr R.J. Finny, an old scholar of Alleyn Court School,Westcliff, of which Mr T.R. Wilcox, B.A., is the Principal. It was in this School that Mr Finney received his early art tuition under Mr James Townshend, R.B.A., who still teaches there.*

Scholarships and Siam *AC Magazine 1930*

Best congratulations to D.M. Nenk on being elected to a scholarship at Haileybury, and also to R.F. Barrow on being elected to one at Cranleigh.

C.B.I. Willey won a Balliol Scholarship last December.

This is one of the best things that an old Alleyn Court boy has ever done, and moreover we believe we are right in saying that he is the youngest Harrow boy that has ever been elected to a scholarship at Balliol. We send him our best congratulations and are confident that further honours await him at his University when he goes into residence there in October, 1931.

Some months ago an old Alleyn Court boy, Tommy Higgins, went out to Siam to engage in the timber trade. Whilst he and another Englishman, together with a large number of natives, were in the forest, cholera broke out in the camp. In the face of great danger, these two behaved splendidly; they sent the healthy natives to another station, remained behind with the sick men, nursed those who survived back to health, and eventually brought them safely to the coast. Well done Higgins, your old School is proud of you. We got this news from *The Morning Post.*

Taking Matron for a spin

Cricket: a Few Short Hints for all the Boys *AC Magazine 1931*

Batting. The right foot (left, if a left-hander) must never be moved in the direction of the leg.

Bowling. Pitch up; never bowl short ones.

Fielding. Be on your toes, and don t put your hands in your pockets or cross your legs.

Catching. Practise regularly every week all through the term.

Wicket-Keeping. Either stand close to the stumps, say, not more than a foot away, or, if you haven't sufficient confidence for this, go two and a half or three yards back; so many boys stand about a yard away, a silly position.

Calling. The hitter calls for everything he hits in front of him, the boy at the other end calls for the rest. The non-caller must say nothing.

Running. Always run the first run as fast as you can, and when you are running a close run, remember to run in with your bat on the ground in front of you.

And a Few DONT'S for the Very Small Boys

DON'T pick flowers or eat grass when you are playing.

DON'T come in for your innings without your bat.

DON'T put your pads on the wrong way up.

DON'T bowl to the batsman when he is looking the other way and admiring the view.

DON'T play with your sleeves down, or your shirt not properly tucked in.

DON'T stand on your head, or turn somersaults during an over.

Night expeditions *AC Magazine 1932*

Mr Richards and Mr Mackie made a good many night expeditions in search of moths, and though nothing particularly rare was caught, were on the whole fairly successful, some of their captures including a Lappet, Fox Moth and two Poplar Hawks. It was found that in quiet roads moths were attracted by a car's headlights, and this was the method they usually employed. Next year it is hoped to rear more moths from caterpillars or eggs, as this is the best and sometimes almost the only way of obtaining perfect specimens of some of the larger and rarer species.

The following Old Boys are at Cambridge:- Cooper, Wilcox, Reed, Savill, Whitehouse, Sherwood, Wykes, Walker, Waymouth, while Willey and Whittard are at Oxford.

Scholarships *AC Magazine 1934*

We were all delighted to see the following paragraph in the *Times* -
> *The Price Entrance Scholarship in Anatomy and Physiology, value £100, open to students of the Universities of Oxford and Cambridge, has been awarded to Mr C. B. Willey, of Balliol College, Oxford.*

It will be remembered that on leaving Alleyn Court, Courtney Willey went to Harrow and from there gained a Balliol scholarship at the age of sixteen. We have just heard that he has taken First-class Honours at Oxford. Many congratulations!

Essex Cricket *AC Magazine 1935*

Nigel Wykes, who is now a master at Eton, took over the captaincy of the Essex County Cricket Eleven when Mr Wilcox was taken ill with appendicitis. Under his leadership the side did extremely well, scoring a great victory over the South Africans.

Nigel Wykes was captain of Alleyn Court in 1920.

Mr Wilcox captained Essex in that historic match against Yorkshire, when Yorkshire were all out for 31 in the first innings and 99 in the second innings.

Letter from Germany *AC Magazine November 1936*

Jenkinson writes this interesting letter from Cambridge:-

Dear Mrs Wilcox,

As you see from my address I am back from Germany and am up here at Emmanuel. I am having an exceedingly good time, but I have not yet waded my way through the literature about all the Clubs and Societies here. I am tempted to join at least fifty – or so it seems at any rate – and the result is I have only joined one – the Union. I am reading Modern Languages and average three lectures a day; two are in the afternoon. I have not actually met any old boys yet but I have an idea I saw Shenstone in a theatre yesterday. As you know I was at Heidelberg last year. I had an excellent time. At various times I visited all the larger towns round there as well as going to Baden-Baden. I also managed to get away to see the Eifel races on the N' rburg Ring. It was raining and foggy all day. I played rugger there in the Winter and Easter terms. I just scraped into their fifteen in the rather surprising position of wing forward. The German players make up for any lack of skill in their size and weight, which they always use to good effect. In the summer I rowed, but that branch of sport is one I cannot stand.

At the beginning of August I migrated to Berlin and stayed there with some people I faintly knew. Here I again had an excellent time, apart from seeing two days of the Olympic Games, the only really important event I saw was the Final of the 100 yards in which Jesse Owens equalled the world's record.

Berlin was, of course, absolutely packed at the time and was so liberally decorated with Nazi flags and country folk from excursion trains, that I hardly saw it at its best. Potsdam and Sanssoucci, being further out, were less crowded and could be properly appreciated.

I saw Hitler on his balcony four times in two days. He had come out about every hour to let the huge crowds, which had gathered on the square and the street in front of his house, see him. He did not speak but simply stood there – long enough at any rate to to make my well practised arm ache for some time. I hope my letter has not been written too late to cause you any inconvenience. And in concluding I should like to say how much I hope Alleyn Court are doing as well as they always have done. I shall be delighted to read of their doings in the next magazine.

Please remember me to Mr Wilcox and to any other members of the staff who are still at A.C.

Yours sincerely,
Bruce Jenkinson.

Basil Grant *AC Magazine 1938*

We received a delightful letter from Basil Grant, who is now practising medicine in Putney. 'Two things reminded me that a letter was long overdue to you,' he writes. 'Firstly the announcement in the papers of Denys's engagement; and secondly a performance of *The Pirates of Penzance*. This was the first time I had seen it performed by the D'Oyly Carte company, and it was an evening of memories for me; memories of the dear late Mr Wilcox shouting from the wings in rather more than a stage whisper "Louder, Louder!" of Godfrey as the Major General; of Archer as the Sergeant of Police; and lastly of my own thrill when, owing to a last minute defection of one of the Keys brothers, I was co-opted to the chorus and had the great privilege of spending a complete evening immersed in a beard.'

A world champion table-tennis player *AC Magazine 1938*

Once again we were privileged to have a world champion table-tennis player exhibiting his wizardry in our school hall this term. Bergmann, the Austrian, was our guest this year. We are indebted to Stanley Proffitt, the English Swaythling Cup player, for these annual exhibitions.

Denys Wilcox at the Oval in 1938.
Denys married Phyllis (above) in
the same year

Stanley Richards
preparing
for Sports Day

Entomology for the Schoolboy

By J.R. Fowles (Div. 1a) & D.L. Erwood (Div. 1b)

British butterflies and moths are not nearly so large or multi-coloured as some of those from tropical countries, but some of them are quite pretty and all are interesting.

First of all, let us consider the stages before the insect becomes a butterfly or moth. There are four of them, firstly, the egg which is laid by the female, secondly the larva, commonly known as the caterpillar, thirdly, the pupa, or chrysalis, and lastly the imago (the perfect insect).

Butterflies, on account of their colours, are perhaps the insects most generally admired; however, some of the moths, such as the Hawk family, are extremely colourful.

The majority of the moths are nocturnal. There are several ways of catching them, but it is obviously useless attempting to do so with a net alone, as some of them are very swift on the wing. One method is to mix honey and beer together to form a paste and then smear it on a fence or tree. The moths, attracted by the honey, will sip it up and the beer will intoxicate them so that they will be unable to fly. Another, and by far the easier, method is to shine a lamp in the open, the moth, drawn by the light, will circle round it, then it can be easily netted.

Having caught the insect, there are various ways of killing it. The ordinary way is to put it in a bottle containing a small quantity of cyanide. If this is not available, crushed laurel leaves will do just as well.

A few last words of advice to beginners. When you are setting a specimen, be patient, for it may not be possible to obtain another one.

Extract of a letter from Nigel Gordon Wykes, formerly an Alleyn Court pupil and Essex cricketer who was a housemaster at Eton, when he wrote on September 7th 1942:

My dear Denys

... the problem of education in general is difficult enough as it is. What it will be like after the war, if such a state of things ever comes into being, nobody can say. I have no doubt that money will become tighter and tighter and the more expensive schools will either have to become less expensive – a great deal less expensive (£30 or £40 will make no difference) – or they will go the way of all institutions which refuse to meet the march of time and the so-called progress that goes with it. The public school system, with its rigid exclusiveness, will certainly have to go, the sooner the better in my opinion but I do hope the essential features of its education will survive for the benefit of all pupils who are fit to enjoy it and not for the few whose parents happen to be rich enough. After this war the money will no doubt be there but it will be in different hands, and we shall have to be careful to see that the people who have enriched themselves by this war do not exploit their ill-gotten gains for their own interest. Fine talk, I know, but the means and methods are not so easy to see and will be even more difficult with European Civilisation in the melting pot ...

All good wishes to you and the school and in parting I ask you to remember one thing – that life is just a bowl of cherries.

Yours ever, Don.

One Man's War – A Fight for the Opera

Reprinted by permission of *The Times*, 6 November 2003.

> The story of how a former Alleyn Court boy rebuilt and ran one of the world's great opera houses is one of the strangest of the Second World War. Sixty years on, he tells Richard Morrison how he did it.

A few days after the liberation of Naples a young British Army Officer was strolling through the city's streets when he came across a startling sight. It was a majestic old theatre – locked, silent, abandoned and distressed. A bomb had ripped away its foyer, bringing the roof crashing down. Piles of masonry blocked its grand entrances. Its walls were scarred with bullet marks from the recent battle.

The officer, Lieutenant Peter Francis of the Royal Artillery, had no special knowledge of Italian opera houses. He barely recognised the name on the torn posters among the debris – Teatro di San Carlo. He certainly didn't know that he had stumbled across what is arguably the oldest working theatre in Europe.

Peter Francis as a pupil at Alleyn Court

Even so, he was intrigued. A non-smoker, he produced 50 army-ration cigarettes and bribed Giuseppe, the ancient stage doorkeeper, to let him in. And so began one of the strangest chapters in the history of the Second World War: the story of how a 26-year-old British anti-aircraft officer found himself running one of the world's great opera houses.

Today, Francis (now 86) lives in Poole. In civilian life he became general manager of the Southend Water Company, then took early retirement and went into the travel business – running, among other things, opera tours to the San Carlo. It is 60 years, almost to the day, since he stepped into that theatre. Yet his memory of that moment is as vivid as if it had been yesterday.

The sight that greeted him inside was tragic. Rubble was piled high in the corridors. Dressing rooms and stores were unusable. The famous auditorium was coated in debris and dust, its top balcony largely collapsed. And the stage grid was a tangle of snapped wires and smashed pulleys, the result of Allied aircraft strafing a German machinegun post on the roof.

Francis saw all this by the shafts of daylight piercing the damaged balconies – the electricity supply was dead. Yet his reaction to the magnificent interior, with its glorious painted ceiling and six tiers of boxes, was much like Stendhal's when the French writer had walked into the San Carlo in 1817: 'There is nothing in all Europe which gives the slightest idea of what it is like . . . it dazzles the eye, it enraptures the soul.' Francis was also dazzled and enraptured. 'I said to myself: "What a theatre! We must get it open"' He went to see his brigadier, who took the matter to the area commanders. 'A day or two later the word came back: "Only too pleased; give the troops something to do". And that's how it started.'

Today, the restoration of an opera house takes years (Venice's La Fenice is only now reopening after its 1996 fire). But in November 1943, in a city short of the most basic materials and with the front line just 30 miles away, Francis achieved a sort of miracle. He had the San Carlo open in just two weeks. And, remarkably, he did it without being able to speak Italian ('I'm told I speak it now with a strong Neapolitan accent', he says).

Word quickly got around that a mad young Englishman was trying to get the city's grand old theatre on its feet again. Gradually its former staff, who had been unable to work there for more than a year, drifted back.

'The first to return was a tenor called Ettore Ponno,' says Francis. 'Luckily, he was married to an Englishwoman, so his English was pretty good.' With him as interpreter, Francis was able to round up the old stage crew. 'They were so over-joyed to be back that they worked incredibly hard to repair the stage machinery and lighting.' The most pressing problem was the power supply. 'At that time most of Naples was running on the generators from submarines,' Francis recalls. So he cheekily invited the adjutant general to the reopening gala. As if by magic, the San Carlo was immediately provided with its own generator.

Similar tactics got the foyer rebuilt. 'We needed cement, and the Navy controlled the big cement works. So I promised their top brass some tickets for Gigli singing *Aida*.' The cement arrived *molto prestissimo*.

Wood, canvas and wire were scrounged, begged or strong-armed from around the city. Francis marched a column of troops up to the music conservatory to requisition a grand piano. Squaddies were detailed to clear the debris. The owner of what Francis describes as 'Naples's equivalent of Liberty's' was strongly encouraged to replace the theatre's drapes. Finally, the San Carlo's celebrated front curtain – a spectacular painting of Parnassus by Giuseppe Mancinelli – was brought out of its wartime hiding-place and proudly rehung.

Making the theatre usable was one thing. But then Francis had to find a show to put on. His first notion was to involve Ensa (officially, the Entertainments National Service Association; unofficially 'Every Night Something Awful'). But Ensa quickly decided that running the San Carlo was too big a task. So Francis, undaunted, decided to go into showbiz himself.

He wasn't a complete novice. His father had been a solicitor who numbered Jack Buchanan and other prewar theatrical luminaries among his clients. So from boyhood Francis had known the smell of greasepaint. 'I would have liked to have gone into the theatre, but my father was dead against it. He'd seen how precarious the business was.' Instead, Francis trained as a company secretary and joined Lloyds of London.

But when he was called up in July 1939 (already commissioned in the Territorial Army) he found himself increasingly playing the role of barrack-room impresario. On coastal defence duties in East Anglia he persuaded Ivor Novello to entertain the troops. Then, posted to the Blandford training camp in Dorset, he ran films and variety shows for new recruits. Even when he was in North Africa and engaged in the fierce defence of Annaba, he had helped the composer Eric Fenby to organise an ad-hoc Southern Command orchestra.

Nothing, however, could have prepared Francis for the task of filling one of Europe's biggest stages with nightly entertainment in the middle of the war zone. He reopened the San Carlo on November 15, 1943, advertising 'first-class entertainment for all Allied forces' in a show titled So This is Naples – a saucy revue that must have been a first in the theatre's illustrious 200-year history. Most of the opera orchestra had returned, and on the following Sunday, under the eminent maestro Franco Patané, they gave a concert of operatic overtures and arias – the only music they could lay their hands on until Rome fell to the Allies the following year.

A sprinkling of shows by British military bands and passing celebrities followed. Amazingly, even Humphrey Bogart played the Naples Opera House, though Francis can't remember exactly what he played. But those were mere appetisers. Francis had not resurrected the San Carlo merely to turn it into the

Lieutenant Peter Francis of the Royal Artillery

Golders Green Hippodrome of the south. He wanted it to be a working opera house again. And on Boxing Day 1943, just two months after he had first set foot in the rubble-strewn building, he achieved his goal with a matinee performance of *La Bohème*. Officers were charged 100 lire (about five shillings, or 25p); 'other ranks' 30 lire. *Lucia di Lammermoor* followed that same week. And from then until November 1945, when he returned to England, Captain Francis (he was promoted early in 1944) supervised 713 performances of 30 operas.

So wrapped up did he become in running the San Carlo that he even started to sleep there at night. 'Very eerie it was, too, going back across that dark old stage at midnight. One night I had Cynthia with me (the Wren officer whom he met and married in Naples). Just for fun when we crossed the stage I pulled the cord that started the rain machine. That shook her a bit.'

At first the casts were San Carlo stalwarts – though Francis roped in British troops to fill out the Grand March in *Aida*, and then to play the part of the firing squad in *Tosca* (he took the precaution of checking that they were using blank ammunition). But when Rome fell, Francis suddenly found himself dealing with the likes of Tito Gobbi, Beniamino Gigli, Toti dal Monte — in short, every prima donna and preening tenor in the Italian operatic firmament.

It was a crash-course in both bel canto and big egos. Shortly before the curtain went up on *Aida* one day he received a message: 'Signora Stignani will not sing this afternoon. The soldiers are smoking by her dressing room.' It transpired that a new batch of British soliders had been drafted into the Grand March for the first time. Because most of the dressing rooms were unusable, they had indeed changed their clothes, and smoked, right outside the room allocated to the very grand mezzo-soprano Ebe Stignani.

Francis pleaded with the vastly-proportioned singer. Stignani replied: 'No, you must see my father', and indicated a somewhat sinister figure lurking in her dressing room. 'It was clear to me that they just wanted more money,' Francis recalls. 'So I simply ordered the stage manager to raise the curtain. Suddenly she found that the opera had started. She sang, of course.'

At first Francis put on operas only in the afternoon, because of the fear of air raids. But no air raids came, and Allied troops were flocking to the performances — partly out of curiosity ('the box office did get the odd complaint, along the lines of "where are the dancing girls?"') and partly to impress their new Italian girlfriends.

So Francis started to run operas twice daily. Performing standards, he admits, were variable; there was no time for dress rehearsasls. And the turnover of sets — sometimes four different operas in a weekend, with an orchestral concert on the Sunday night — would have had the stage manager of a modern opera house gasping in disbelief. It didn't greatly impress the San Carlo stage manager at the time, either.

'He came to see me one day,' Francis recalls. '"Capitano, he said, "you really want *The Barber of Seville* in the afternoon and *Turandot* in the evening? It's impossible. I can't change the scenery in time!" So I thought for a moment and replied: "Move the *Barber* sets further down-stage, and then build the *Turandot* sets behind it while the opera is on. Quietly!" If you put your mind to it, you can achieve these things. If you say it can't be done, it won't be.'

By the time that the British Army handed the San Carlo back to the Italians in May 1946, more than 1.5 million Allied servicemen and women had seen an opera there. Francis attributes the extraordinary appetite for opera in postwar Britain at least partly to the 'San Carlo effect', and he is probably right. When the war ended, the San Carlo asked him to stay on as its permanent administrator. He said no. By then Cynthia was pregnant, and he had a job waiting in England. His brief but action-packed career in opera administration ended that day.

On stage at San Carlo. Peter Francis *who today, with the same love, frequently returns*

But not his association with the San Carlo. Shortly after the war the company came on tour to Covent Garden. And as a mark of respect to Francis, its orchestra travelled to Southend on its free evening and played a charity concert in the Odeon. 'Made £300 for the local hospital,' Francis says, 'It was a lot in those days.'

Then in 1993, 50 years after he first entered the theatre, Francis was presented with a plaque in the great auditorium. The inscription read:

> *From the San Carlo to Captain Peter Francis who, half a century ago, dressed in the uniform of the British Army, managed the theatre after the freeing of Naples, and who today, with the same love, frequently returns.*

'It's an odd thing to say about wartime, but those were the most fulfilling years of my life,' he says.

40 Queensborough Terrace,
Hyde Park,
London, W2.
23rd August 1945.

Dear Mr Wilcox,

Thank you very much for your letter offering me the Mathematical post at Alleyn Court. It gives me much pleasure to accept this offer, and I shall look forward to joining you in Devon next term.

Will you very kindly let me know the date on which term starts, and whether you would like me to bring any of the boys down with me. It would interest me, too, to know what text-books are in use at Alleyn Court for the mathematics.

Please excuse this rather hurried note, but I am just starting off for business and would like to catch the early collection.

With kind regards,
Yours sincerely,

Victor A. MacKenzie-Stewart.
Will there be any chance of meeting you in town during the holidays?

Editorial *AC Magazine March 1947*

On a day in September, 1939, a hasty conference took place on a gun site in Essex. Mr Noble had travelled hundreds of miles searching the English countryside for a wartime home. At last his efforts were rewarded, but a quick decision had to be made. Motoring back to Essex, he tracked down Mr Wilcox, the decision was taken, and in a few days sixty boys with gas masks, and not much else, were being escorted to a country house in the heart of Devon.

In spite of the discomfort of those first frantic days, without furniture, it was not long before the beauty of the surroundings dawned upon us. Bigadon House was remarkably like Courteenhall, near Northampton, which was the home of the school in the first World War. Though without gas or electricity we soon became accustomed to our new conditions. About the six years we spent there much could be written, of anxiety and difficulty, of happiness and success, and no editorial could fully tell the story. But we can say that the traditions of the school were worthily upheld. A high standard of work was maintained and scholarships were won with encouraging regularity. On one of the fields near the house a concrete cricket pitch was laid and a football field marked out. Matches were played and our teams were often the victors. And we must not forget to thank those kind friends in Buckfastleigh who did so much to make our time of exile happy. When at last we returned to Westcliff we found the familiar pink cap very much in evidence, for the day school, under Mr Noble, had reached substantial proportions in spite of the many difficulties. A year has passed since then, and now that we have settled down we must look to the future.

Bigadon House in Devon, Alleyn Court's home during the Second World War, seen as it was (left) and as it became (below)

1940 *AC Magazine March 1947*

> *M. Desternes, Head of French at Alleyn Court, was in France when*
> *the Germans overran the country. He fought later with the Free*
> *French Forces. We have asked him to write an account of the*
> *Germany entry into France.*

En moins de soixante-dix ans, trois fois les Allemands ont envahi la France.

La première invasion, si grave qu'elle eût pu être, n'était que la conséquence de défaites purement militaires et devait s'arrêter dès que la France aurait donné satisfaction à l'Allemagne: cession de l'Alsace et de la Lorraine et paiement d'une indemnité de guerre.

La deuxième invasion visait à la destruction de la France ellemême. Elle fut infiniment plus brutale comme peuvent en témoigner les habitants du Nord et de l'Est ayant vécu sous la bottle allemande durant quatre années. Les Allemands se livrèrent à dés atrocités, à des exécutions en masse d'otages, à des viols, à des vols et à des réquisitions multiples dont celle des hommes afin de les envoyer aux travaux forcés en Allemagne.

La troisième invasion fut de loin la pire de toutes. Grâce aux armes modernes, la guerre de tranchées, statique, interminable, ne pouvait se renouveler, et le front étant percé, rien ne pouvait plus s'opposer au déferlement des armées ennemies sur toute la France. Les Allemands s'inspirant de cette théorie, celle de celui qui allait devenir un de nos plus célèbres généraux, se dotèrent d'une forte armée motorisée qui n'eut pas grand peine à défoncer les faibles lignes françaises et anglaises en trois semaines environ.

Qui se trouvait en France à cette époque se souvient très bien des routes encombrées dé réfugiés, de femmes, d'enfants, de civils, de militaires en déroute, de soldats sans officiers, d'officiers sans soldats, de voitures de toutes sortes, et le tout copieusement arrosé de bombes et de rafales de mitrailleuses pendant des jours et des jours et sur des centaines de kilomètres. Tout ce troupeau était poussé par l'armée allemande qui arriva même à s'infiltrer si loin que les réfugiés bien souvent n'allèrent pas plus loin, comprenant fort bien que les Allemands ne s'arrêteraient qu'aux Pyrénées.

On vit alors une multitude de side-cars, de chenillettes et de tanks. Des camions, énormes et puissants, trainant de massives remorques, répandirent rapidement dans nos villes et nos campagnes des flots de soldats, jeunes hommes et même adolescents, fiers d'être victorieux, et qui, respirant la santé, défilaient dans nos rues en chantant.

'Il n'y a pas à dire, ils sont organisés' disait-on de toute part. Et ce contraste avec notre laisser-aller fit, que quelques Français furent plein d'admiration et d'enthousiasme, et oublièrent que dès lors notre liberté devenait une chimère et que notre vie même dépendait du bon plaisir de ces "messieurs" (comme on disait alors). Partout les "feldgrau" se distinguaient par leur correction, leur politesse, voire même leur galanterie à l'endroit des dames. Ils allaient dans tous les magasins, achetaient n'importe quoi et payaient largement sans compter... avec notre monnaie! Ils essayaient de lier conversation et pensaient nous consoler en nous affirmant que la question de l'Angleterre serait règlée dans une quinzaine de jours. Ils se montraient aimables et parfois même serviables.

Aussi, à l'exception des habitants du Nord et de l'Est qui les connaissaient bien depuis 1870 et 1914 et qui déclaraient déjà fin juin qu'ils n'avaient pas changé, bien des Français furent trompés par ces apparences.

Car, qui aurait alors pu faire croire que ces mêmes hommes allaient quelques mois plus tard, affamer les Français, leur prêcher la résignation, les déporter, les assassiner, les fusiller, après en avoir horriblement torturé par l'intermédiaire d'une police dont les pratiques rappellent celles des temps les plus reculés? Et qui aurait pu croire qu'il y aurait des 'Maillé' et des 'Oradour' comme il y eut des 'Lidice'

Et qui prouve qu'il n'y aura pas d'autres 'Lidice' et d'autres 'Oradour' en Europe – ou ailleurs – si nous laissons ces gens – là se relever de leurs ruines comme ils s'en sont déjà relevés une première fois?

G. Desternes,

Ex-S./Lieutenant Free French Forces

'Varsity Football *AC Magazine March 1947*

Congratulations to Trevor Bailey on his soccer 'blue'! Playing at outside-right he scored two goals for Cambridge in the 'Varsity match thus repeating the performance of another Old Boy, K.H.L. Cooper, who also scored twice against Oxford playing in the same position.

The Music Club *AC Magazine March 1949*

Report of Meetings during the Autumn Term

All the five meetings were well attended, there being about 50 boys on each occasion. During each meeting one of the records in the series 'The Young Person's Guide to the Orchestra' by Benjamin Britten, was played and explained. The term finished with a programme devoted to carols and Christmas music, a number of these records being lent by the boys.

Mr Weston conducts the meetings and gives us many interesting explanations and pieces of information that would not normally come to light.

We have all enjoyed the Music Club and I am sure we all look forward to many more happy meetings.

R. A. Bulgin,
Hon. Secretary.

Appointments *AC Magazine March 1949*

We congratulate: A.J. Holladay on his election to a Fellowship of All Soul's College and his appointment as Lecturer in Philosophy at Wadham College, Oxford; C.E. Macdonald, who has been appointed Lecturer in Classics at Sydney University; J.H. Bishop on his appointment as Lecturer in Classics at St. Andrew's University, D.H.J. Hilary, who has achieved this outstanding record; at 12 he won the First Scholarship to Tonbridge, at 13 he gained his School Certificate with five distinctions, at 15 he took the Higher Certificate and gained a distinction in classics, at 16 he gained his second Higher Certificate and was the first among 120 entrants for a scholarship examination held by a group of Cambridge colleges; in the Higher Certificate he was placed second of all candidates taking the examination.

Founder's Hall *AC Magazine March 1949*

As to out-of-school activities, the new School Hall takes pride of place in our interest at the moment. With much enthusiasm we are watching it rise, brick by brick, slowly taking shape and form, and growing into an edifice that will surely be worthy of its dedication as a memorial to the founder and first head-master of the School, Theodore Robert Wilcox.

Founder's Hall, as it will be called, will instil new life into the more social side of our activities. In the past, the full realization of many of our plans has been hampered by lack of the necessary accommodation and amenities. Founder's Hall will remedy all that. Here we shall have an assembly hall with all the necessary fitments and appurtenances for its use as lecture hall and cinema; gymnasium (with boxing ring and physical training appliances); playroom, headquarters of school societies: and, last but not least, a theatre for the performance of Christmas entertainments. It will, in fact, be the pivotal centre of the general school life, and as such should give a decided impetus to the successful achievement of our aims. It will be in Founder's Hall that each day will start with the Assembly for Morning Prayers.

AC Magazine March 1949

For the Edification of Parents who are likely to play Marbles during the holidays

Now that the marble craze has asserted itself again, parents are likely to be pestered for 'just one game of marbles.' Without an elementary knowledge of the rules, they are likely to be caught unawares. We are therefore publishing a glossary kindly provided by members of Remove A.

'Keepses' and 'Lendses' Before the game it is decided whether to play 'Keepses' or 'Lendses' This determines whether the player, hitting his opponent's marble, keeps it or gives it back.

'Rebounds' – It is decided also at the start whether to play 'Rebounds'. This means that if a marble is hit by the other marble on the rebound, it may or may not be won according to the decision.

'Stopses' – If a player calls out "Stops," he may stop his marble from rolling at the position when he called.

'Dropses' – If he calls 'Dropses' and if his marble is within the distance between his outstretched feet, he may drop his marble from thigh-height and try to hit his opponent's marble.

'Liftses' – When a player calls 'Lifts' he is allowed to play his marble over any intervening object.

'Fudging' – A player is said to have 'fudged' when he plays his marble in front of its former position.

'Clearses' – If he calls 'Clears' he is permitted to remove any article which is likely to hinder his shot.

'Bombses' – When 'Bombses' is called, the player may throw his marble from about chest level at his rival's marble.

* 'Tipses'– If the marble is not hit full face, the player whose marble it is may call 'Tipses' and the marble will not be won.

* 'Roundses' – If 'Roundses' is called, the player may shoot round an interfering object by swinging his arm round it.

'Nothings' – If before taking a shot, the opposing player shouts out 'nothings' the player about to take the shot is not allowed to make any of the above operations, except for 'Stopses' and 'Liftses'.

'Everythings' – If, on the other hand, the player playing the marble calls 'Everythings' before his opponent cries 'Nothings' he can perform any of the above rules.

* Theses are only minor rules, and may be omitted.

From the Diary of a Schoolboy's Fountain Pen *AC Magazine March 1949*

June 26th

Spent last night on the cricket field in the pouring rain, if you please! This fellow, Johnson minor, my present owner, is the absolute limit; I might be a common dip-pen for all the care he takes of me. I've had a streaming cold in my nib all day; as a result, he is very cross with me because my ink flows too fast. I had a frightening experience this morning: I was put in a foreign pocket and was jolted against a foul-smelling box of tobacco, then I was held up in front of all the boys. Eventually Johnson minor came and claimed me. I think I have got influenza (atishoo). I am not going to write any more.

G.H.L. (aged 13)

Cricketers in the Making   *AC Magazine April 1951*

Last August, Hutchinson published *Cricketers in the Making*, a book for cricket coaches and schoolboys, written by Trevor Bailey and Mr Wilcox. The book has been very well received by all sections of the Press. The brilliant photographs taken by Mr Charles Bruce have undoubtedly been a major factor in the success of the book.

These, as the *Daily Telegraph* says, 'set a new standard.'

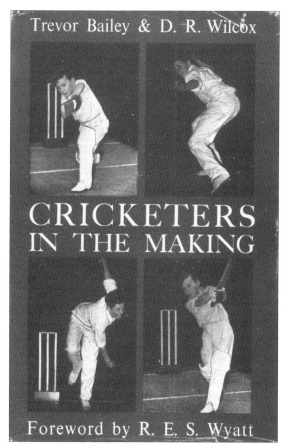

Momentarily the
centre of the
cricketing world

The Fiftieth Anniversary 1904-1954 *AC Magazine 1952*

In just over twelve months the School will be celebrating its Fiftieth Anniversary. To mark this great occasion the Old Boys have formed a Committee which is to launch an Appeal for funds to build changing-rooms and baths on the playing field. The School is not well equipped in this most important respect, the present accommodation being quite inadequate for the number of boys. It is intended that the building, which will be a permanent structure, should also serve the purpose of a pavilion.

The Committee is as representative as possible of the fifty years of the School's existence and will make its appeal to all other Old Boys, parents past and present, and friends of the School. Only once before has such an appeal been made. This was after the first World War when parents and friends built the Memorial Passage designed by Sir Charles Nicholson.

The Committee intends to send out the Appeal in the New Year. It feels that there is a fund of good will towards the School and is confident of the success of this great project. Until the appeal is formally launched the Committee asks that subscriptions should not be sent. It is realized, however, that considerable initial expense will be involved in printing and stationery, and any practical help in this respect would be greatly appreciated.

The composition of the Committee is as follows. The names are given in chronological order, the dates signifying the member's time at Alleyn Court.

H.D. Rankin	1910-1914	(Alleyn Court and Haileybury)
N.G. Wykes	1914-1920	(Alleyn Court and Oundle)
R.O.G. Norman	1917-1925	(Alleyn Court and Rugby)
F. P. Francis	1925-1930	(Alleyn Court and Bradfield)
G.G. Shenstone	1926-1931	(Alleyn Court and Tonbridge)
T.E. Bailey	1932-1937	(Alleyn Court and Dulwich)
H.J. Verney	1931-1938	(Alleyn Court and Stowe)
D.H.J. Hilary	1935-1945	(Alleyn Court and Tonbridge)
D.F. Austin	1936-1946	(Alleyn Court and St. Edward's)
J.H.P. Maley	1945-1948	(Alleyn Court and Charterhouse)
R.A. Bulgin	1945-1949	(Alleyn Court and Westminster)

Of Reading *AC Magazine 1952*

Ask a man in these days whether he reads much, and all too often the reply will be something of this sort: 'Not much. An occasional thriller. I never get the time.' Or, 'Only thrillers. They exercise my mind and give me just the mental stimulus I require.' Or even a candid, 'nothing, really, other than the newspapers and a periodical or two.'

The fact is that in a not inconsiderable section of the community reading, in its wide, cultural sense, seems practically to have disappeared.

That this should be coincident with the spread of education must give us pause. Perhaps the general change of attitude towards leisure and the place it should occupy in our lives has a good deal to do with it. More and more we have come to regard leisure as a preparation for work, a time of rest and recuperation in which we gather strength for renewed effort in our chosen career, a necessary factor for producing the maximum weekly output. This was not the view of the old Greeks. They regarded work as a preparation for leisure. 'We busy ourselves about many things,' one of them wrote, 'so that we may enjoy our leisure.'

Are our lives any the happier for this change of emphasis? I think not.

For most of us our times of leisure are our main opportunities for the acquisition of culture. Reading in its broad sense (I am not concerned with reading in preparation for examinations or for advancement in our profession) is the foundation of culture. Without culture a man is incomplete; his inner life lacks wholeness; his outlook is narrowed and restricted within the limits of his own experience; he lacks within himself a certain indefinable power of self-contained sufficiency – not the self-sufficiency that makes a man consider himself better than his fellows, but one which gives him a wider sympathy and a greater ability to understand and appreciate them. 'Reading maketh a full man,' wrote Francis Bacon.

What are we schoolmasters doing to guide taste and choice in the rising generation, so that our boys may at least have the opportunity to share in this wider life of the spirit?

One item of young people's reading that gives rise to a great deal of controversy is the popular 'Comic.' My own view is that, within reason, a desire to read 'Comics' – or 'Bloods,' as we elders knew them – is a quite normal phase in the development of the average youngster. Attempted repression is, I am sure, wrong. In any case it is almost certain to fail. I remember hearing of a Preparatory School where 'Comics' were banned absolutely, and severe penalties laid down for reading them. For many terms all seemed to be going exceedingly well; 'Comics' reading appeared to be a thing of the past. Then one night several dormitories had to be evacuated at short notice, and a staggering number of 'Comics' were found under the mattresses!

No; repression is certainly wrong. Of course an undue absorption in this class of reading is to be deplored, for it is likely to sap the strength of true literary appreciation. But the contention of psychiatrists, that children must experience the various stages of development in order to pass beyond them, strikes one as sound reasoning and in accord with normal growth as we know it in Nature. 'Comics', in my view, are one of the stages.

There we must leave it for the moment. Let us not fail to take seriously this matter of helping our young folk to attain a fuller consciousness through the approach of Literature.

Life is meant to be more than an incontinent scramble for bulkier pay packets. There is a life of the spirit that is to be found and enjoyed only in times of leisure. Knowledge comes in the Silence. Be still, then, and know.

And remember the children.

V. A. Mackenzie-Stewart.

Quiz *AC Magazine March 1950*

Give the answers to the following:-

1. What word meaning 'more than enough' contains two E's, two S's, an X, and a C?

2. Can you find an 'unlucky accident' in consecutive words of this sentence NOW TOM IS HAPPY AT HIS WORK?

3. Can you re-arrange the letters of SHAPE DICE to make the name of a famous Street in the City of London?

4. Can you make the letters of TRUE APPLE into a word which means 'continuous'?

5. In the sum:- $2A3 \div 7 = 29$, what figure does the letter 'A' stand for?

6. Can you name three fish from these:

   LERMCEAK   LAIBUTH   LEAPIC ?

7. Can you make a young dog into a Scholar by adding two letters to its tail?

8. Can you make DUEL DISH FRED into a Yorkshire town?

   J.M. Rolling.

A prize of a book-token will be awarded to the first boy to hand a correct answer to Mr Gotch.

Food for Thought *AC Magazine March 1950*

The writer of the following article, Raymond Cusick, for a while Art Master at Alleyn Court, subsequently made his name as designer of the Daleks for the BBC.

You may think, to what extent does all this affect us? It may seem on the surface to appear rather remote. Just how important is the purpose of Art to us? And by the term Art, I mean it in its widest sense to embrace all forms. Anything fashioncd with man's hands where some aesthetic judgement on his part has had to be made in its formation or construction. In fact, anything from a piece of pottery to a building). Does it have any bearing on living and making living more enjoyable? Well, it does. We cannot escape it; in fact we need it. It is all around us, if we care to take notice. It is part of our way of life and thought, a cornerstone in the structure we call civilization. Even if we do not take an active part in creating, most of us have a share in participating as an audience. Art enhances life, like a jewel fashioned from the rough stone of existence. It is not meant to be an imitation of life, but a statement on what man thinks about it. It is food for the mind, which we need just as much as we need food for our bodies. The more mental energy we use up the more we need to replace it.

Many materialistic people think that Art is a luxury, like icing on a rich cake. They think it is an appendage that costs extra money. And it is true that a beautiful piece of carving is useless to a starving man, but if the man is not hungry, but well fed, and then has nothing to think about, what then?

When at school we try to learn the fundamentals of knowledge. When we finally leave school and face life we realize the possibilities and scope for its enjoyment. Armed with our little knowledge we learn to develop it along paths that suit us individually. Some of us want to understand more about life, which is the occupation of scholars and artists. The artist's understanding arouses certain emotional feelings and attitudes which he tries to express in books, plays, music and art. They give to the rest the mental food, or energy stimulus that is so necessary to a cultivated and civilized mind.

R. P. Cusick

A Visit to the House of Commons *AC Magazine 1952*

Thanks to the courtesy of Mr Bernard Braine, MP, the Head Boy accompanied a member of the Staff on a visit to the House of Commons.

During May, 1941, a German bomb crashed through the roof of the House of Commons and the Chamber was burnt out. The four walls were left, scorched but sound, to withstand the ravages of the weather for four years until the enemy was beaten into surrender. Only then was the task of reconstruction undertaken.

The new House has lost nothing of the character of the old, which was built in 1834, and has gained considerably in other respects. It is now possible to hear every word spoken whether it be uttered by a Back Bencher or a Minister.

Ruth Wilcox: A Tribute by John Paddy Carstairs *AC Magazine March 1956*

How lucky the child to be in the right hands in the all-important time of early adolescence!

I was one of the lucky ones; three wonderful women administered to my needs, guided and contributed greatly to my well-being and happiness. My mother, naturally, Mrs Noble and Mrs Ruth Wilcox.

Dear Ruth! What a warm and radiant personality over-flowing with the milk of human kindness, sweet natured and gentle. How well she cared for us at Alleyn Court. I will always be grateful for her affection and her understanding. At Alleyn Court my brothers and I – four of us – came under her spell, she was so cheery and she made it all so cosy at a time when we were (having been spoiled of course!) very homesick. But one could not be homesick for long. Ruth Wilcox made Alleyn Court a home-from-home. What I shall – and I am sure I write for hundreds of old Boys – always remember is her cheeriness, her strong sense of fun and her old-world courtesy – such a rarity these blustering, uncouth days!

We, too, will always remember laughing with her and not at her – for you don't laugh at people of whom you are so very fond – those gigantic hats – one was positively fearful she might 'take off' in a high wind and she would have been the first to laugh – and, of course, that delicious old dog of hers – Bobbie.

It would be wrong to say Ruth has gone, Ruth will always be with us, her silent presence watching over Alleyn Court – what a splendid family the Wilcoxes! Theo and Ruth and Denys, their memory shines like a Bright Star over the School and the Field they all loved so well. They gleam in our memory.

John Paddy Carstairs made his name as a film director, novelist and artist. He directed the Norman Wisdom films and exhibited at the Royal Academy.

Editorial *AC Magazine June 1957*

At Easter we lost two good friends. Mr Noble gave up the Headmastership after many years of faithful service by himself and Mrs Noble to Alleyn Court. We are glad to say that they are settling near the School so that the break will not be complete, as Mr Noble will still be with us teaching some forms.

It has been a year of ups and downs. The competition for entry to the Public Schools is now so fierce that boys from all schools are finding it increasingly difficult to cope with the Common Entrance Examination. The only answer is hard and steady work for the whole four-year course.

Once again the Cricket XI were unbeaten. This makes the fourth unbeaten season since the war. The Football team has improved greatly as is witnessed by two drawn games with Southend High School, the first time we have avoided defeat from them at least once in a season.

Ernest Noble who worked as Joint Head with both the founder and Denys Wilcox

This term Mr Dyer has taken over as Headmaster. We extend to him and Mrs Dyer the heartiest of welcomes. We are confident that they will see to it that the Alleyn Court flag is kept flying high. Mr and Mrs Dyer have had much experience of Prep School work and will bring great experience to their task. We know that they can count on the loyal co-operation of boys and Staff.

At a small ceremony held at the end of the Easter term, Dr Norman presented to Mr and Mrs Noble a television set on behalf of the Old Boys and the Staff. Mr Richards presented them with an inscribed silver gilt bowl on behalf of the boys.

I am terribly sorry that I had the insolence to use my peashooter on you.

Miss Chandler

Alleyn Court,
Westcliff-on-sea
Essex

Dear Miss Chandler,

I am sorry that everybody stares at you, and abuses you. I am also terribly sorry that I had the insolence to use my peashooter on you, and I can almost swear that I will not again. The reason for everybody is staring at you is to make you see that they think you very attractive.

your affectionate admirer

Visit to Tosca *AC Magazine 1962*

During the latter half of the Autumn term two visits to the Sadler's Wells Opera House were arranged by Mr Michael Wilcox with the view of helping boys with their Scholarship General papers. One party went to see Puccini's melodrama *Tosca* while the other, comprised mainly of boarders saw Johann Strauss' *Die Fledermaus.*

It was a cold, blustery Saturday afternoon that several boys, looking unusually smart, Mademoiselle Delerue and Mr Wilcox, were transported by car to Southend Victoria and thence by train to Liverpool Street.

After an ample meal at a small restaurant a stone's throw from Sadler's Wells, we took up our seats in the Opera House. *Tosca*, our programmes told us, was to be played by Victoria Elliott, and Baron Scarpia by Owyn Griffiths. The stage sets throughout were lavish and produce a strong sense of atmosphere. I can remember little, unfortunately, of the costumes, except that *Tosca*, who was, as is often the case, a little plump, wore a crimson dress which trailed behind her as she swept across the stage, and that the villain wore appropriately a suit of black. I think it was agreed by all that the second act, in which Baron Scarpia is murdered, was the most dramatic and even the most enjoyable. Although I am no judge of singing, it was commended by no less an authority than Mademoiselle Delerue.

Certainly this was opera in its grandest form and I feel sure that we were all encouraged by this outing to take the next opportunity to watch an opera.

S. N. Jolley. (aged 12)

A new dining hall AC *Magazine 1964*

The improvements to the school buildings continue. The new dining hall is now in full operation, and is much admired by Old Boys, one of whom (his Public School shall be nameless) said he wished theirs was half as good!

A new covered way has been built connecting Nos. 3 and 5 for use in wet weather. This also obviates the constant traffic through 1B form-room. A new entrance into the changing room, next door to the new lavatories now solves the traffic problem of 1A form-room.

The old junior dining room is now a televison and common room for the boys during the day, and the staff during the evening.

The new gas heating engine in No. 1 is working most reliably and keeps the form-rooms in No. 1 beautifully warm.

It will interest some present and some old boys that Mr Cusick is now working for B.B.C. Television. In fact, he designed the Daleks in 'Dr Who.'

Good Morning Mr Bradman: Editor's note

The article which follows is reprinted from *The Cricketer* and is included because it makes reference to a number of significant Alleyn Court characters. Our own Trevor Bailey, who played in both the 1948 and 1964 encounters with the Australians in Southchurch Park, these matches being the original subject of my article, has always generously acknowledged the influence of Denys Wilcox who somehow combined the roles of young headmaster and Essex cricket captain in the 1930s. Trevor was also to become Essex captain and more importantly one of England's greatest all-rounders. Together they wrote *Cricketers in the Making*, a coaching book illustrated with outstanding photographs by local photographer Charles Bruce using Alleyn Court boys as models, and organised the first residential course for cricket coaches ever held. One report remarked that Alleyn Court had become momentarily the 'centre of the cricketing world'. Household names in the world of cricket came to Westcliff to share their cricketing wisdom and experience.

We should not forget other Alleyn Court internationals. Simon Clarke, scrum-half for Cambridge, Blackheath and England, Julian Halls, winner of numerous international caps for the England hockey team, Ken Cooper, an amateur soccer international for England in the 1930s and Stewart Robson who made his debut for Arsenal a few days after his seventeenth birthday and who remained an automatic choice for Arsenal, West Ham and Coventry City until injury brought his playing career to a premature end. This was not before he captained the England Under 21 team and a full international cap seemed only a matter of time.

Trevor Bailey

Mark Foster, the world record-breaking swimmer, is another notable former pupil athlete and there are many other international and county sportsmen too numerous to mention individually.

A love of sports and games was one of the founder's many enthusiasms and this characteristic still manifests itself within Alleyn Court today. Paul Hart, our current head of P.E. has enhanced this tradition.

Simon Clarke

Stewart Robson

Julian Halls

Good morning, Mr Bradman *The Cricketer*

Former Essex player, John Wilcox, reminisces on the county's contrasting encounters with the Australians of 1948 and 1964. Alleyn Court characters include: Trevor Bailey, (the author), Denys Wilcox, Ruth Wilcox, Mr Adams and Mr Mackenzie Stuart.

In a three-day match it can seem a very long wait with your pads on. The Australians were in the field and not responding with much fight to seeing their bowling attack caned to all parts of the ground by Barker and Fletcher. The rest of the Essex batsmen sat in the shade and watched with growing pleasure. It was just the sort of day a captain longed to win the toss and bat on, for South-East England was enjoying a heat-wave and another intensely hot day was in prospect. The wicket was easy-paced with the ball scarcely bouncing stump high, though there was likely to be growing turn for the spinners as the match progressed. The tourists had just won the Test series against England without losing a match. Maybe the celebrations, or complacency, would take their toll. A crowd of more than 10,000 filled Southchurch Park and began to sense that something unusual was beginning to happen.

The minds of many went back 16 years when, on the same ground, the Australians had batted first and made a world record day's total of 721 all out. It was small comfort to the Essex players that they were the only team that season to dismiss Australia in a single day. On that occasion I had just had my eighth birthday and had watched the day's play with my family. It was such occasions that shaped my childish ambitions and preoccupations, so to sit now, waiting to bat in the self-same fixture 16 years later seemed an entirely natural progression.

Memories of that day in 1948 when Bradman's team came to Southchurch Park were as fresh in my mind as if it was yesterday.

My brother and I were to go with my grandmother. She was an inveterate cricket watcher, not surprisingly, since her only son had grown up to be captain of the county. Our father, therefore, sat in some reserved tent, and chatted over old times with colleagues. Our places, as nearly behind the bowler's arm as possible, were always faithfully reserved by Mr Adams, a tall and solemn gentleman, well known to us as the lesson reader of our church and invigilator of exams. In a biblical epic by Cecil B. deMille he would have been cast as an old testament prophet, so normally one would never associate him with error of any kind, but rumour had it that during Test matches he had been known to round off his Sunday reading with 'Here endeth the first innings.'

My grandmother owned and drove a black Hillman Minx. This was part of the day's entertainment. She drove it cautiously except when a storm was in the offing. Only in these circumstances did she throw

Don't you know I'm the best driver in Southend?

caution to the winds and show almost no regard for any other road user. Once a young police officer arrived at the school, which she and her husband had founded at the beginning of the century, to allege she had crossed the traffic lights in Hamlet Court Road at red.

'What disgraceful rubbish! Don't you know I'm the best driver in Southend?' He soon retreated.

But generally she erred on the side of caution and drove with the hand-brake on, which was clearly safer. She grew used to the smell of burning which she regarded as a strange eccentricity of that particular engine.

It should be added in fairness that she generally arrived at her destination, on this occasion the members' entrance at Southchurch Park, and, moreover, in plenty of time for the start of play. The members' car park and temporary safety lay beyond.

An official approached the drivers's window and beckoned somewhat impatiently that grandmother should wind it down.

'Are you a member, madam?'

'Of course I am,' she replied.

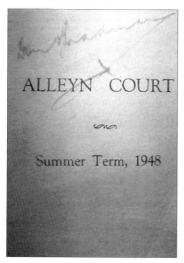

ALLEYN COURT

Summer Term, 1948

Don Bradman's autograph on the 1948 fixture card

'May I see your membership card then please, madam?'

'Yes, of course... if you think that's necessary.' She fumbled in her bag knowing knowing perfectly well that she'd lost it weeks ago. 'Where is the wretched thing?'

A queue of cars began to form behind us. Drivers put their heads out of their windows and made encouraging remarks to the gateman. He began to feel under more pressure than grandmother.

'I must have left it at home! What a fool I am! Don't you know me? I've been a member for years and years.'

The official looked around for a colleague.

He was in luck.

''Ere... Fred. Come over here a minute.'

We waited for Fred.

Before he arrived he knew the situation.

'Good morning, Mrs Wilcox. Keeping all right are you?' And without waiting for a reply, 'We'd better get you in quickly hadn't we? Quite a queue building up... pity your son's not playing still... Carry on then, dearie.'

A mixture of relief and indignation showed itself on the old lady's face as she drove into the car park.

'Fancy calling me dearie, cheeky man.' She edged up to the car in front slowly. Her signal to stop was when she felt contact.

'I don't think you ought to leave it touching ... couldn't you back a bit?'

I said this because she hated backing; finding reverse was always a great problem to her. At last she managed it accompanied by an agonising sound of wrenched metal.

'Oh, now what's happened? Be a dear and get out and see.'

Unluckily the bumpers had entwined and we had half pulled off the rear bumper of the car in front.

She got out and surveyed the damage. 'Oh that'll be all right... not that bad... I've some wire in the boot. We'll tie it back on.'

After the wire came baskets of food, binoculars, cameras, rugs, coats and umbrellas. Also trailing along on the ground a fox fur, of disgustingly moth-bitten appearance, which lived in the car, crouching on the floor in front of the back seat.

'Good morning, Mr Adams. Were you able to keep us some seats as usual?'

Mr Adams raised his hat with stately deference – as the hats had met exactly the same number of times as their wearers he had had plenty of practice – and indicated three seats.

'Good morning Mrs Wilcox. Here you are. I've been here since before 10 o'clock to make quite sure.' And so the ritual began.

In fact, that day in 1948 had been more like a ritual slaughter, the victims being the Essex bowlers. Grandmother firmly believed that a little walk would cause a wicket to fall and so my brother and I were often despatched for this purpose. Invariably we went to the pond behind the pavilion to watch the boats, throw pebbles or try to spot fish lurking in the murky depths.

Denys Wilcox with his sons John (left) and Michael

Wickets did fall but in the middle of an avalanche of runs. Donald Bradman came in 20 minutes before lunch and was approaching 50 when the umpires took off the bails to signal the interval.

My Dad arrived. 'Come on John, I want you to meet someone.' He looked around in vain for my brother who had disappeared.

Approaching the pavilion we stopped when a small cricketer in a green cap approached us.

'This is Mr Bradman, John. You've just seen him batting haven't you?'

'Yes... I have.' What more could I say?

The Australian bent down and took my hand.

'Hello, John. Are you going to be as good a cricketer as your father, d'you think?

'I don't know, sir. I hope so.'

'The best of luck to you, anyway,' and after a few more words to my father he was off to the lunch tent.

An appeal rang out and merged with the responding murmur of the crowd, bringing me back sharply to matters in hand. Umpire Price's finger went up. Only one more wicket and then it was my turn to bat.

'Good luck, John,' said a voice that sounded familiar.

Another voice from the past... that of Mr Mackenzie-Stuart whom I had not seen since he had taught me English at about the age of 11.

'Thanks a lot... see you later I hope,' I added, realising that he knew it wasn't the right moment to wait around for a chat.

We had loved his teaching, especially the afternoon lessons when he read to us. Coming in from an afternoon break in summer I remembered, our shirts sticking to our bodies with the exertions of our games on the field, he wisely knew lessons late in the day did not provide ideal opportunities for comprehension exercises or the analysing of sentences.

Instead he read to us his favourite poems and stories, and did so with such enthusiasm and style that it amounted to the best teaching he ever did, in my belief. Slight and frail but with a twinkle in his eye he had a good Scottish voice with one unusual characteristic; on almost every 's' or soft 'c' his voice would whistle, and sometimes so piercingly that we would lift our heads from where they rested on arms and desk lids and wink to our neighbour or special friend as much as to say, 'That was a good one, wasn't it? Thus 'the silence surged softly backward' sounded rather like a dawn chorus.

Another appeal echoed round the afternoon ground... but, of course, it is the voices of childhood that echo longest and from them there is no escape.

But enough of this... my turn to bat at last!

In 1948, the Australians won by an innings and 451 runs in two days after hitting 721 on the first day. Sixteen years later Essex won by six wickets – with two Alleyn Court boys in the winning team.

Election Day *AC Magazine 1965*

On the day of the General Election the Senior and Middle Schools met to elect a representative of their own. For a week beforehand notices had been seen everywhere exhorting electors to vote for this or that one of three voluntary candidates: only these knew which of the three National Parties each represented, chosen by lot. Meanwhile, the parties were known generally as A, B and C.

In the afternoon of Election Day a grand meeting was addressed by the three candidates, who each sought to set out, in terms of the School, the policies of the National Party he represented.

E. Bundock (A), in a wittily composed and admirably delivered speech, promised many reforms, without modifying the existing general form of the School. The reforms were to be paid for by fines and taxes, from which the Staff would be the chief sufferers! I. Pell (B) was much more sweeping – not to say vigorous – in his promises of re-constitution, prep. not escaping the axe. A. Littman (C) quietly assured his hearers that all was well and that little change was needed, but he was astute enough to agree with those of his opponents' projected changes which the audience had seemed to favour.

There followed questions from the body of the meeting, and numbers of the younger boys were among those who had points to raise.

Finally a vote was taken with this result:-

Party C   62 (Conservative)

Party B   52 (Labour)

Party A   25 (Liberal)

This is an interesting result when one considers that it was not until after the poll that the electors were told the real identity of the three parties so that they had to judge solely by the policies outlined.

School Notes: Miss Mingay   *AC Magazine 1966*

At the end of the Christmas Term Miss Mingay retired from teaching at Alleyn Court. Unfortunately all good things come to an end. During the war years the School evacuated to Devon and in 1944 again opened up in Westcliff for day boys. It was then that Miss Mingay joined the staff.

From that day until the day she left, she was always the guardian angel of all the boys beginning the adventure of school life.

This remarkable lady had that quality that inspired the respect of both the boys, and the people with whom she worked. No matter how great the crisis, her voice was never raised, and a few kind quietly spoken words of reassurance saved more than one boy from breaking into tears.

She will be remembered by so many Old Boys who realise what an important part she played in their early school days. In fact she possessed the qualities that go to make the loved and dedicated schoolmistress.

As she is living in the neighbourhood no doubt Miss Mingay will come to Alleyn Court from time to time. These visits will be greatly looked forward to by all at Alleyn Court.

Extract from *Essex Countryside*   *AC Magazine 1968*

From Australia:

> I do not know the Wake Arms near Epping (March issue), but reading about the inn reminds me of the moves Alleyn Court Preparatory School of Westcliff made during World War I owing to the German air raids, first to Englefield Green in Surrey and then to Courtenhall, the Northamptonshire home of Sir Hereward and Lady Wake.

I was one of the boys who went with the school on its war-time travels and can still remember the thrill we all felt at living in the home of a descendant of such a history-book hero.

G. H. Brett,
14 Roma Street,
Bentleigh, SE14,
Victoria, Australia.

Mr Richards *AC Magazine Easter Term 1969*

School Notes: Mr Richards this year completes the remarkable record of forty years splendid service to the school. While on this subject it is interesting to note that eight members of the staff have now completed a minimum of ten years service each.

Visits: Rev. Browell gave a further talk and film on Dr Barnardo's Homes.
Mr Chevenix Trench gave a film on Fishing.
Mr G. Whaite gave a talk and film on Banking.
In July we had a most exciting visit from a R.N. Helicopter (Westland Wessex), which landed on our field, much to the excitement and, in some cases, perturbation of some local inhabitants! Rumour was rife! The crew, after giving a spectacular exhibition of life-saving at sea (the sea being our field!), disembarked and, converting the Founders' Hall into an up-to-date cinema, showed films and slides and answered many questions.

Mr and Mrs Noble have left Westcliff and settled in Minehead, Somerset.

Oil heating *AC Magazine Easter 1970*

The new oil heating system that has been installed is really wonderful. Never before has every corner of the whole school been heated. The heating comes on well before school and all classrooms get the benefit.

Southend Poetry Trophy *AC Magazine 1971*

In the Southend Poetry Trophy G. James won the 1st prize in the under 12 age-group and was the over-all winner. His poem is published elsewhere in the magazine. A. Silverton was 2nd in the under 12 age-group and D. Bawtree was 3rd in the under 18 age-group.

The work of the following boys is to be included in a book, 'Young Poetry', to be published by the Pulin Publishing Co, of Wales: T. Hannah, A. Blake Milton, D. Mallett, J. Howard, D. Muir, G.P. Thomas, D. Bawtree, J. Deacon, G. James, A. Silverton and J. Nichols. We must apologise to any boy who has now left the School if his name has been omitted.

During the summer holidays an Anthology of boys' work, illustrated by Mr Richards, was published. This was a great success and it is hoped that a second Anthology will be produced this year.

A new activity for the Seniors in the evenings this year has been the Drama Class taken by Miss Lovegrove. The boys seem to enjoy these classes and we look forward to the fruits of their labours at the end of the Summer Term.

Prefects: Autumn 1970: A. Facey (Head Boy), N. Watson, S. Pinkerton, M. Button, J. Deacon, A. Bishop and D. Muir. Spring 1971: D. King, D. Hughes, N. Havens, W. Murphy, D. Bawtree and D. T. Thomas.

Presentations: We should like to thank Mr and Mrs Furner for the Staff Room clock; Mr Facey, Mr Wiggins, Dr and Mrs Michell, Mr and Mrs Bird, Mr and Mrs Docherty, Mr and Mrs Young, Mr and Mrs Taylor and Mr and Mrs Timms for donations to the Library; Capt. and Mrs Pascoe for Blades and Fencing Gloves; Mr Trench for a cup for the Butterfly Stroke in Swimming.

AC Magazine 1971

The Golden Hind

There she stands, her sails furled,
Set in a concrete keel.
Does she dream of the open seas,
Billowing canvas and salty spray?
Or does she prefer her sheltered home
With her silent crew of wax,
Hearing no more the sailor's oaths
But children's laughter on her decks?

Graham James (aged 10).

H. M. Herman

Many Old Boys and friends of the School will have already learnt with regret that Mr Herman, who came to Alleyn Court in 1947, has recently been unwell and has retired from teaching. Though he visits the School regularly and we see much of him, in our day-to-day life we miss greatly his unfailing kindness and loyalty and his many contributions to School life not only in, but outside the classroom; the editing of this magazine is but one example. Many boarders, too, will remember his cheerful early morning greetings, followed instantly by a sharp reminder that it was high time to 'rise and shine', given with an enthusiasm inspired perhaps by the thought of breakfast and *The Times* crossword waiting downstairs. They will remember also a schoolmaster with the rare and happy ability to command obedience and affection in equally large measure.

Hermie is now living at Priory House, Prittlewell Chase, where he enjoys enormously meeting or hearing from his many friends.

Eileen and Stanley Richards *AC Magazine Lent 1974*

After 45 and 46 years respectively, Mr and Mrs Richards have retired. Needless to say these are the longest careers in the history of the school, spanning the offices of every headmaster this school has had.

It was in 1927 that Mrs Richards, then Miss Kidgell, came to Alleyn Court, to be followed the next year by Mr Richards. In the light of subsequent events one wonders whether this was entirely coincidental! At any rate in 1937 they were married and the Richards had arrived.

Now it is not easy to express what these two people have meant to this school and the many hundreds of boys who have come and

kindness, perseverance and goodness: Eileen and Stanley Richards

left. Let me express it like this. If one looks very closely at a painting, perhaps one of Mr Richard's, one can admire each details in isolation – the skills of the artist, the technical expertise displayed. But standing back the wonder of the whole transcends the sum of the particular parts; it is only then one can appreciate the unity of the whole, the artist's certainty of purpose.

Similarly in these two careers we remember the skill of two teachers, their example of courtesy, their loyalty and kindliness, Mr Richards' ability as a games player and artist, and the way he communicated his knowledge and enthusiasm to countless boys.

Yet together they have meant more to Alleyn Court than the sum of all these qualities combined; they too have given to everyone here a sense of unity and purpose. Reading through the many letters from Old Boys which accompanied their contributions, it is very clear what they felt. This is a part of just one of them: 'Over the years I have come to realise how much I owe to their kindness, perseverance and sheer goodness in my formative days. I was lucky to have them as teachers.'

Dolphin Camps *AC Magazine 1975*

These camps, which are well supported by Alleyn Court boys and Old Boys, provide holidays appropriate to the various age ranges and interests from which they cater.

The Senior Activities, such as Wray Castle and Kart Camp, admit boys from the age of thirteen, taking Public School boys, and some of the Alleyn Court boys who are in their last year here.

The Junior Camps, held at West Runton in Norfolk, cater for Preparatory School boys in the eleven to thirteen age range. This year members of the School have taken up all of the 30 available places, almost all being booked by Christmas.

Old Boys Notes *AC Magazine 1976*

Ken Hervé (1962-1968) is to be congratulated on winning the World Championships in the Hornet Class in Perth, Australia in January. This achievement completed his hat trick, having won the European title at Thorpe Bay last July and the British title at Herne Bay in August. Unfortunately he and his crew member are unable to go on to attempt an Olympic gold as there is no Hornet Class in Montreal.

School Notes *AC Magazine Lent Term 1977*

It may be of interest to note that since the School's foundation in 1904 boys from Alleyn Court have entered no less than 130 different Public Schools. The most popular, statistically, no doubt for geographical reasons, are Felsted with 323 entrants from Alleyn Court, 80 to Bishop's Stortford, followed by Brentwood 65, Framlingham 53, Haileybury 43, Tonbridge 39, Dulwich 35, Epson 28, Aldenham 26, Malvern 25.

The Three Kings that came in the Snow *AC Magazine 1977*

He groped his way through the suburbs. The houses formed a broken line against the blackened sky. The moon was absent, and the pavement was frightened by the late step. He found a plank, already brittled by the Russian winter. It broke across his bony knee with a resounding crack and a flurry of snow. The wood smelled rotted and sweet. He held a piece under his nose. Here at last was some wood, he thought, now he could warm his freezing wife. He groped his way back home. There were no stars.

The door whined as he stepped inside, and an icicle fell from the public tap outside, sending millions of tiny glistening fragments of glass in every direction.

The pale blue eyes of his wife looked towards him. They came from a tired face. Her breath clung white in the room; it was so cold.

He pointed to the wood he had found. 'Almost smells like cake', he laughed softly.

'No,' said his wife, 'Don't laugh. He's asleep.'

The man placed the sweet rotting wood into the small tin stove. There it flamed up and cast a handful of warm light onto a tiny round head. The face was only an hour old but it already had everything that belongs to a face; ears, nose, mouth and eyes.

The mouth was open and a gentle puffing came from it. The nose and ears were red. He lives, the Mother thought. And the little face slept.

The man took some more of the soft wood. Now she's had her child and must be freezing, he thought. But whose to blame? When he opened the door of the stove another handful of light fell over the sleeping face. The woman said softly; 'Look, it's like a halo. Do you see?'

Halo, he thought. And who's to blame?

Then there were some people at the door. 'We saw the light,' they said, 'from the window. We want to sit down for ten minutes, there's a blizzard brewing up.' They saw the child and said nothing more; but they came into the room all the same, breathed mist through their noses and lifted their feet high. Then the light fell on them.

There were three of them. In three shabby uniforms. One had a cardboard box, one a sack. And the third had no hands. 'Frozen off,' he said, holding up the stumps. One of them had his feet in thick wrappings. He took a piece of wood out of the sack.

'A donkey,' he said, 'I carved at it for seven months. For the child. And here's some tobacco for you.'

They lifted their feet high and looked at the small sleeping face. The third man was trembling in his uniform. He took some chocolate out of his cardboard box and said, 'These are for your wife.'

'Thank you,' the man said. 'But what's wrong with his feet and what's wrong with you? Why are you trembling?'

They did not reply. The baby began to cry. They lifted up their feet and crept to the door; then they went.

'Fine, but queer saints', he thought. 'But who's to blame?'

'But my son is crying,' the woman said mournfully. 'No, I think he's laughing.'

'Almost like cake,' said the man and smelled the wood, 'like cake, quite sweet.' The door blew open. A bitter wind entered the room. Three corpses lay by the tap.

'Why it's Christmas today,' shivered the woman.

'Yes, Christmas,' mumbled the man standing over the bodies; and from the stove a handful of light fell on the little sleeping face.

David Atkinson (12 yrs). David subsequently won a scholarship to Felsted.

Camels *AC Magazine 1977*

Camels are endearing creatures and girls especially seem to love them. They are also unusual; they can kick in any direction and spit extremely accurately. They always have a very superior expression on their faces, and it is said that whereas holy men recite the 99 names of Allah, only the camel knows the 100th name.

Camels have many little friends!

From *Boys' Contributions*.

Sir Kenneth Cork *AC Magazine 1977*

Parents and Old Boys, especially those who remember their being chief guests at Sports Day, 1977, who wish to join us in congratulating Sir Kenneth and Lady Cork on his becoming Lord Mayor of London, and in wishing them a very successful year. Sir Kenneth, it will be recalled, spoke with enthusiasm of his days as an Alleyn Court boy, and brought with him the original pink cap.

Mr Dyer *AC Magazine Lent Term 1981*

It is difficult to imagine someone better equipped to be a Prep School Headmaster than Keith Dyer, both by temperament and talent. His own interests and accomplishments encompassed all aspects of school life, the academic, the cultural, the athletic. The successes of the gifted were given proper recognition, to those in difficulty constructive sympathy and encouragement. In courtesy and un-selfishness there was leadership by example.

constructive sympathy and encouragement:
Keith and Freda Dyer, 1957-1981

Old Boys News *AC Magazine 1983*

We congratulate Timothy Hinton, Andrew Latham and Jason Phillips on being appointed Head Boy at Harrow, Felsted and Brentwood schools respectively.

Congratulations also to Toby Walsh on being awarded a scholarship in Natural Sciences at Cambridge.

It has been a good season for Stewart Robson who was appointed England Youth Captain, and who is now a regular member of the Arsenal 1st team.

Michael Wilcox's new play opened at the Lyric Studio, Hammersmith, at the end of February. Set in a prep school in the holidays it is entitled 'Lent'.

Congratulations to David Mackay on being appointed Captain of Football at Brentwood.

Robert Bonallack (Haileybury), with his partner, won the Public Schools Under 15 Rackets Championship at Queen's Club. Paul Titchener was again a finalist in the Public Schools Rackets Championship also held at Queen's.

Old Boys News *AC Magazine 1984*

We extend our congratulations for four Old Boys who successfully took the Oxbridge Scholarship examinations before Christmas.

Simon Hayley gained a place at Wadham College, Oxford to read Philosophy, Politics and Economics.

Christopher Mills won a scholarship in Mathematics to read Economics at St. John's College, Cambridge.

Julian Scarfe won a scholarship in Natural Sciences to Pembroke College, Cambridge.

Afzal Zaidi, who was only 16 at the time of the examination, won a place at Caius College, Cambridge to read Medicine. He is at present assisting in our Science Department.

The British Theatre Association voted Michael Wilcox 'Most promising Playwright' of 1983, an award made for his play 'Lent'. The staff attended a performance of this sensitive and nostalgic play when it was presented at the Dixon Studio during November.

Congratulations to David Atkinson and Jeremy Hayes who were elected to Westminster as Members of Parliament for the constituencies of Bournemouth East and Harlow. David was our guest at Sports Day in July.

We would also like to congratulate Mark Nelson-Griffiths on his appointment as Captain of the British Fencing Team. He first studied the sport under the careful guidance of Mr Hill.

Palace-Go-Round *AC Magazine 1985*

We have been pleased to receive two visits from the 'Palace-Go-Round', the first in May last year when they performed 'Inspector Quaver's Musical Case' and the second in February of this year with their production of 'The Poacher's Lament'.

Two of our pupils have been involved in productions at the Palace Theatre recently as you will see from the photo section of this magazine. Our congratulations to Mark McCarthy and David Quentin on their successes.

Last May we opened the Stanley Richards Study Centre in Kilve, West Somerset. The opening was held to coincide with the inaugural weekend when a group of boys from the scholarship class visited the centre. Already forty-four boys have stayed at the centre, using it as a base for studies in Geography, Geology and Ecology. In addition to this, of course, a stay at the centre, albeit brief, helps the pupils to learn to live together and enjoy some of the beauty to be found of God's creation in this lovely part of the country.

Michael Wilcox, the writer, and John Thaw during the filming of *Last Bus to Woodstock*. This episode of *Morse*, shown first in March 1988, was watched by 12.2 million viewers

School Notes *AC Magazine Lent Term 1986*

Preparations are now well in hand for the introduction next September of a pre-prep department attached to the School. The department will comprise two classes of up to twenty children, each with two teachers and run according to the Montessori Method. It will accommodate children from three years and upwards, and at the present time is fully booked for its first term. A number of structural alterations have been necessary as it is planned to house the new department in specialist equipped classrooms. We look forward to this exciting new development in the life of the School and welcome Miss Phillipa Braybrook, Mrs Suzanne Neale, Mrs Brenda Ruskin and Miss Emma Wilcox as our pre-prep teachers. The latter, the headmaster's daughter, is the prime mover behind this exciting development.

a teacher of genuis:
Marguerite Delerue

On the 8th September last, old boys and teaching staff gathered to pay tribute to a teacher of genius Mlle Delerue. The event was held to mark 37 years of service to the School. All who have sat under her tutelage would want to thank her for the dedication and effort which she has given over those years. The climax of the occasion was the presentation of a cheque and three volumes of the latest edition of Bordas' 'Dictionnaire des Litératures de Langue Française'.

Mlle Delerue writes: 'I am still thinking back with happiness and gratitude to my marvellous party of last September. I am sad, though, not to have been able to contact personally all 'my old boy-friends', all my friends, who contributed to it with such overwhelming generosity. I will never forget. Your wonderful gift will always be a lasting reminder of many happy days in 'Our School', and will prove so useful when, relunctantly, I retire... Merci à tous, et du fond du coeur! 'F.F.'

Boys on stage and screen *AC Magazine 1987*

You will be seeing one of our pupils on TV soon. Ian Harris (7 years old) begins filming soon for his role in BBC TV's production of *Vanity Fair*. Ian is no newcomer to drama having first appeared in a Harold Pinter play at the Palace Theatre in 1985. Last summer he was again at the Palace, in *Lark Rise to Candleford*.

Also treading the boards last Christmas in Pantomime were James Butcher, who played the Lame Boy in *The Pied Piper of Hamlyn* at the 'Cliffs Pavilion' and William Fuller, who played one of the Lost Boys in *Peter Pan* at the Palace Theatre. Marcus Jones also appeared in *Peter Pan* as one of the Indians.

6-a-side *AC Magazine 1987*

The outstanding feature of the football season was the 3rd successive triumph in the East Anglian Preparatory School 6-a-side Championship from an entry of 21 teams. Such a feat has not been achieved by any other school.

Old Boys News *AC Magazine 1989*

We were interested to note that our two old boy Members of Parliament both defied a three-line whip to vote against the government on the related issues of free dental and eye checks. Indeed Jerry Hayes (Harlow) was one of the organisers of the rebellion. He and David Atkinson (Bournemouth East) were two of thirty-three Conservative members to vote according to their consciences in this matter.

James Bourne of *Busted*, Alleyn Court's first chart-topping former pupil

David Hilary *AC Magazine 1989*

David H.J. Hilary, first cousin of a previous headmaster Denys Robert Wilcox, is now Receiver for the Metropolitan Police. We understand that this rather obscure title indicates that he is the senior Civil Servant in charge of 'The Met'.

Old Boys News *AC Magazine 1990*

Mr Wilcox had a letter from Mr Everett, the Headmaster of Tonbridge who is retiring shortly, thanking Alleyn Court for sending so many outstanding boys to his school, and noting what a 'profound'influence for good they had exerted in the academic sphere particularly.

The Southend Head Teachers' Asssociation asked to come to Alleyn Court and hear something from Mr Wilcox, Mr Bishop and Mr Green about how an independent school was run. They felt it was relevant as 'local management of schools (L.M.S.)' is almost upon them and they found the implications worrying. They left professing to feel somewhat reassured!

Reprinted from *The Times Saturday Review* 1991

A Childhood: John Fowles

by Walter Ellis

John Fowles as Essex Man is not a thought that springs immediately to mind. Yet Fowles, the past master of ambiguous fate, is not from Dorset – or Devon – and did not, in fact, set foot in his most familiar milieu until he was 13 years old. He was born 200 miles to the east, in the self-consciously suburban world of Leigh-on-Sea, and grew to adolescence in an ordered world of Home Counties reticence, in which his father wore a bowler hat and left each morning for London on the 7.52.

John Fowles

Leigh, a largely Edwardian creation, lies in a cranny of the Thames Estuary, just west of Southend, looking across to Canvey Island and, more distantly, Sheerness. It was a London overspill development more than a resort, suspended uneasily between city and country and owing allegiance to neither. Fowles, resident in number 63 Fillebrooke Road, went through the greater part of his childhood not knowing Exeter, Taunton or Chard, but Billericay, Basildon and Rayleigh.

Today, as readers of his recent attack on the grockles who infest his town each summer will have been reminded, he lives in Lyme Regis, in an elegant Regency home. Lyme, setting for *The French Lieutenant's Woman*, is perhaps Leigh as it was originally intended; its hinterland is as far removed from the Essex marshes as Wigan Pier from Mansfield Park.

Fowles's father, Robert, had intended to become a solicitor, but had his training curtailed by the first world war. By the time he returned from the trenches, his own father had died and the family business, a small chain of cigar makers and tobacconists, was in trouble. Suddenly, filial piety was everything. All hopes of a career in the law were dashed, and Robert was obliged to devote himself instead to the routine of retail sales.

In 1925 he married Gladys Richards, and soon after they moved to Leigh, where John was born, on March 31, 1926.

From the tranquility of Lyme Regis, sequestered from an enquiring public by the proprietorial protection of its townsfolk. Fowles remembers the circumstances of his childhood with a novelist's clarity.

'My father had wanted to be a lawyer, as massive and sarcastic and rude as F.E. Smith (later Lord Birkenhead), but in reality he was in social ways a timid sort of person. One of the things I remember most is the sight of him growing apples in our garden in Leigh. Every corner of the garden was full of trees producing fruit of a taste and quality I have never experienced since. These misshapen trees were his life, helping him to compensate for what he thought he had lost.'

Fowles's mother, now in her nineties, was a good wife and mother. Her husband was not always the easiest of men. 'He could be moody and overbearing, and she dealt with it well. She was very gentle, and I feel the more creative side of me comes from her, just as my emotions come from my father. But she was conventional, too. I can express all sorts of things that must have been repressed in her. When I wrote erotic passages in my books, the conventional side of her would disapprove, but somehow I feel her deeper, more atavistic side would understand.'

As a small-time manufacturer and retailer of 'luxury' items, his father had to struggle in the difficult economic conditions of the Thirties. An uncle, who was a master at Alleyn Court school, in Westcliff, had managed to get John admitted on a reduced-fee basis, but the result was that he felt 'only tolerated' by both staff and pupils. 'I knew how they viewed me – we were never poverty-stricken, but we were on the brink – and this worried me.'

Fortunately, there was someone at Alleyn Court who cared, Denys Wilcox, its headmaster, a former Essex cricket captain, 'was the man who really began to make me have confidence in myself'. He encouraged Fowles to play cricket – soon to become an obsession – and supported him in his studies, so that he eventually won an exhibition to Bedford School.

Home, meanwhile, was a semi-detached, mock-Tudor villa, tantalisingly close to the beginnings of the Essex woods and fields. An uncle, who used to 'sugar' moths – trapping them on a cloth smeared with honey – introduced Fowles to lepidoptery, a hobby he practises still and exploited in *The Collector*. Young John was mesmerised. Another relative, Lawrence Wetherall, his cousin, was a first-class field naturalist. Forays into the marshes with this amiable eccentric were highlights of Fowles's early life.

With the coming of the war and a perceived threat to the south Essex coast from Goering's bombers, events took a dramatic turn. The family moved to a relative's cottage in Devon, between two farms in Ipplepen, near Totnes, and were to remain there for the next three years. Fowles recalls the shock of the change. 'I'd say I was happy until the age of 14. But when we got to Devon I realised suddenly that there were far more shadows in life than I had realised.' A kind of nervous breakdown ensued, possibly connected with the fact that he was about to be sent away to school, and it was chiefly his mother's loving care which saw him through this unexpected depression.

Devon itself was a revelation. In Daniel Martin, his partly auto-biographical account of a civilised Englishman reviewing his past, Fowles paints a vivid picture of a way of life which, although seemingly undisturbed by the ravages of war, was about to come to an end. His descriptions of a harvest in 1942 could have come out of Hardy; the fiery arrival of a Heinkel bomber, on its way home from a raid on Dartmouth, is the one ominous hint of the disruption to come.

Fowles spent his long school holidays in Ipplepen and quickly deepened his already profound love of nature. 'I came from the suburbs and I think the suburbs and the country are so opposed. My discovery of plants and animals and real country people, completely different from the wretched middle-class world of my previous experience, was wonderful.'

Simultaneously, he became aware of the sharp social distinctions that existed in rural society. Birth, he observed was 'irrationally important' and the signs of breeding were indelibly marked. The boy in Daniel Martin, 'shy and ashamed of his educated dialect', is the author – wanting to be friends with the 'real' people around him, unable to do so because of his assumed privilege and unwanted patina of accent.

The reality was his father with duodenal ulcers, his mother taking in 'paying guests' and himself turning into 'a determined little poacher', catching any bird or fish that would help fill the family larder. There was also the added responsibility of Hazel, John's sister, born in 1941.

School created its own hazards. 'We were fighting Hitler abroad, but at Bedford we were in the grip of the Gestapo.' Discipline was traditional and strict. Fowles turned out to be 'a disaster' in the marine corps and took little interest in rugby. Yet he was obviously bright and a talented cricketer, and ended up as head of school. Why he accepted that role, he cannot now understand. He remembers only that he was absurdly conformist.

There was also, of course, the small matter of girls. Readers of the Fowles oeuvre will be aware that sex is never far beneath the surface of his novels. At Bedford, however, it was so deeply entombed as to require almost forensic exhumation. 'Like all boys at that time, I was terribly sex-starved. People today can't imagine what it was like. I don't know how we led such repressed lives.'

A trial, then, but he survived, and with the end of hostilities and a return to Essex, a long childhood finally receded. Ahead lay Oxford, and a long and happy relationship with Elizabeth, his wife, who died two years ago of cancer. More distant, but drawing him inexorably, lay the exotic landscapes of France and Greece, so vital to his development as an artist.

It could have been so different. It probably was. Some say he played cricket for Essex and helped win the Gillette Cup, others that he sold the family business and acquired a Ford dealership in Basildon, where he still lives. It is even rumoured that he personally revived bare-knuckle fighting in Romford and gave snooker lessons to the young Steve Davis. Who knows? Writing is one thing, but John Fowles could have been a contender.

Alleyn Court School
Imperial Avenue,
Westcliff-on-Sea.

7th February 1992

Dear Parents,

This is another letter in a series advising you of our continued search for a larger site. I have negotiated the purchase of the freehold site known as Eton House School – dependent upon the successful sale by tender of the present Alleyn Court playing field. The outcome of this sale will be known in late March and you will be informed immediately.

Allow me very briefly to tell you why this course of action has been adopted – for after all there is a part in all of us that would like things to stay just as they are. (I say briefly for if these transactions go ahead I will be setting aside a number of evenings at Alleyn Court when further details can be given and I will be available to answer your questions about them).

Firstly the kind of school we need to develop to meet changing demand cannot be contained within the four acres presently at our disposal. (The Eton House site is more than three times as big and further land may be available as and when required). Alleyn Court's founder chose as a motto 'Non progredi est regredi', not to go forward is to go back, or to put it another way, to merely stand still is not good enough. The idea implicitly encourages us not to be afraid of change. Two of his great grandchildren still work in the school, the fourth generation to do so, so there is no lack of continuity or sense of purpose.

If we are about to embark on a great undertaking I have complete confidence that all working together can accomplish something of lasting value. We'll wait and see and I will write again as soon as more is known.

With all best wishes.

John Wilcox.

Old Boys News *AC Magazine 1993*

Mark Foster

In February this year Mark Foster became the fastest swimmer in the world, lowering the 50 metre freestyle record to 21.60 seconds. He also set a world record of 23.72 seconds by winning the 50 metre butterfly at a World Grand Prix meeting in Leicester.

The former Alleyn Court pupil, now 6ft 6in, travels five evenings a week from his home in St. Neots, Cambridgeshire, to the Barnet Copthall club in North London to train under Dougie Campbell. He also undertakes three mornings a week training in Kettering, in addition to serious weight training.

He will compete with Alexandre Popov, the Russian gold Medal winner in Barcelona, in the long-course 50 metre pool, at this summer's European Championships in Sheffield. Now his four-year goal is gold in Atlanta, an objective to which he confidently aspires.

PC or not PC: Computer Room Refurbishment *AC Magazine May 1998*

We are immensely grateful to the ACEH Association for their grant of £4000 from monies raised at last Summer's Champagne Ball. It provided just the boost we needed in order to completely refurbish the computer equipment in the Main School. I am certain that everyone will be only too keenly aware that, when purchasing items of this nature, the pace of change is such that equipment bought has been superceded before it has been unpacked. It was decided not to place too high a premium on the speed of the processor but to ensure that sufficient machines were bought to enable every pupil to have individual access during their computer lessons. We therefore opted for twenty-one P133 Multimedia machines one of which is also equipped with a Modem, allowing Internet access and the sending and receiving of email. The total cost of the refit was in excess of £14,000, which I believe to be excellent value for money.

Excuses *AC Magazine 1998*

Current excuses	Future excuses
My pen ran out of ink	My batteries were flat
I couldn't find my Prep diary	I saved it but couldn't remember the file-name
I've lost the book	My hard-disk crashed
I hurt my arm and couldn't write	My printer wasn't compatible
My brother spilt tea over the work	My brother spilt Coke over the keyboard
I've left it at home	I've left it at home

Julie Turner *AC Magazine 1999*

So I close with the words of Haim Ginott, which are food for thought, for all who work with children:

> I've come to a frightening conclusion that I am the decisive element in the classroom. It's my personal approach that creates the climate. It's my daily mood that makes the weather. As a teacher, I possess a tremendous power to make a child's life miserable or joyous. I can be a tool of torture or an instrument of inspiration. I can humiliate or humour, hurt or heal. In all situations, it is my response that decides whether a crisis will be escalated or de-escalated and a child humanized or dehumanized.

Julie R. Turner.

Girls *AC Magazine 2001*

In April 1993 we moved on to the new site previously occupied by Eton House School and the decision to admit girls into the Main School was taken. This was something the Wilcox family had wanted for some time but the restricted space on the previous site made it impossible. The admission of girls has been an unqualified success. They have, in my opinion, a very civilising effect on boys – it is no coincidence, for example, that the Alleyn Court of today is much less volatile than the Alleyn Court I rejoined in 1990. The girls have made the school a healthier place and it can only be a good thing, both educationally and socially, that the boys and girls learn to coexist naturally.

The decision was also taken to take pupils through to GCSE. With hindsight this was wrong because, although our GCSE candidates gained outstanding grades, Alleyn Court's history has been all about preparing pupils for the secondary school of their choice and there were not sufficient numbers staying on to make it viable. The closure of the Senior part of the school was probably the lowest point in my working life. Not because it was the wrong thing to do but because of the consequences for those directly affected. Since then the school has re-established itself as the town's premier Preparatory School where pupils can be prepared for entry to secondary schools anywhere in the country – no other school can open so many doors.

William Wilcox.

Members of Parliament *AC Magazine 2001*

David Atkinson MP has become the first backbencher to address the United Nations. He spoke on the subject of co-operation between the UN and the council of Europe.

Andrew Tyrie MP was voted backbencher of the year by *The Spectator*.

Editorial *AC Magazine Lent Term 2002*

This is an especially poignant editorial for me, as it will first be read on the day that I leave Alleyn Court. I will go remembering not the few frustrations, but the many happy times and fascinating characters that I have so enjoyed over the last four years. Alleyn Court has more than its share of interesting people: it is an environment in which individuality and enthusiasm thrive. Most of my teaching has been concentrated on Year 6, and each year has brought an amusing and entertaining group of children who develop new jokes and themes. It is also true that for every time I despaired about the structure of a letter, I was surprised ten times by the ideas and originality of people so young. My only regrets are that, inexplicably, Southampton FC, *Star Trek* and *Dad's Army* have attracted no new followers, and that some people still prefer J.K. Rowling to J.R.R. Tolkien.

I've also taught alongside an array of fascinating characters, some of whom have already left. The stories I could tell! Many children who leave have written back to say that things are not quite the same elsewhere, or about how well Alleyn Court prepared them for Senior School. I have always edited this remark out from the 'News of Former Pupils'. Now I also fall into the category of someone who has learnt a lot while at Alleyn Court School.

I always felt slightly embarrassed that it was my name linked with this magazine when the effort was so widespread, and the children so self-reliant and inventive: in essence, my job was to glue and paste! Thanks must go to Jane Hendry for spending so much time proof reading. She has an eye for the tiniest detail and rooted out more mistakes than I thought possible. Likewise, I am grateful to all those who contributed photographs. Thanks also to those teachers who prepared sections or articles: I hope that my editing has done justice to your work. Last but not least, Modern Graphic Arts, the printers, have again been professional and tolerant – thanks!

Most of all, thank you to the children. Many have contributed, and all are mentioned somewhere inside, even if just in the form list. This editorial has had a personal tone, which I regret: the children have made Alleyn Court what it is, and this magazine, I hope, gives some idea as to why teaching them has been such an enjoyable, rewarding and amusing job.

Tom Burden.

Dear Richard *November 2003*

Letter received from Campbell Whalley (now resident in Australia) on 3rd November 2003. Photographs of Campbell feature in the front cover of Cricketers in the Making *bowling and fielding.*

Dear Richard, [Chandler]

This I fear, will be an inadequate thank you for all the time you gave us the other day... Friday, 17th October. It was quite an experience for me to re-visit the old Alleyn Court school buildings that I remembered and it was very comforting to see so much of the old boarding area still very much in use and happily so. It would seem to be an ideal situation for the very youngest members of the Alleyn Court community to start their schooling. I'm not sure as to whether or not I actually gave you any information that you didn't already know as to the layout and use of the various rooms but it was fascinating for me to see them again and to see them otherwise used. I can't begin to count the hundreds of hours worth of table tennis that we watched with Mrs Wilcox, senior, in her sitting room above the front door. Television was very new in 1946 and 'Programmes will be resumed as soon as possible' was forever on the screen. But, with our pyjamas, dressing gowns and a few extra blankets besides, we made toast with Mrs Wilcox while we waited for Victor Barner(a)? to get going again. The Staff Room, as you well know, held very special memories for me! because in 1946 until 1950 at least, it was the Matron's room. This was another room in which we made toast at the gas fire after our baths across the landing. It was in this room that we listened each evening to the next episode of Dick Barton and from time to time to 'Itma'. I was probably the only boarder who slept in that room with the matron... it is not half as improper as at first it may sound... in fact, it was quite the opposite. My parents were trying to make telephone contact with me from Peru and after two days and nights it still hadn't been made. It did require, however, that I was close to a phone all night and the matron, Miss Winstanley, must have drawn the 'short straw'. Contact was never made. Denys Wilcox came up to the room early on the third morning and put a halt to it... the little fellow, in his opinion, had had enough. It was not difficult to remember each room because it was very much home to about fifty or sixty of us. Food rationing was 'full on' but we were fed well and it must have been difficult to feed such a large number. We played lots and lots of cricket and soccer and this became a very important part of our happy boarding days. We certainly worked in the classroom and there must be plenty of evidence to back this up. We walked the Southend Pier at regular intervals and were taken to the County Cricket matches. In 1948 we were taken to see Essex play the visiting Australians. By the end of the first day, Australia had scored 721 runs! The only success for Essex was K.Miller bowled T. Bailey for 0... everybody else seemed to get at least a hundred. Trevor Bailey brought us back to school that evening and we were a little late by 'Chads' reckoning. I remember her displeasure, quite well, and I guess Trevor Bailey might remember it also... poor man, he had been bowling his heart out all day against, argueably, the best batting line-up of all time. As boarders, we adored Denys Wilcox and we thought his wife (Mrs Denys as we called her) was 'SMASHING'... the two of them seemed to enjoy the boarding boys. The one other area of the old school that I remember well, although we could not visit it on this day, was where, I think, you said John Wilcox 'makes camp' when visiting. This was the San. and also the room in which we took our Common Entrance Exams! I remember it well because it was in this room that I spent the first two weeks of the 1948 summer holiday. It happened this way... the school would breakup and about six of us ('hang-overs') from the 'Devon Days' would stay on another night and would then be taken down the next day to the West Country by Stanley Richards. During that night I went down with Chicken Pox. My guardians had their own school at Ilminster and so I had to stay at Alleyn Court. As luck would have it, the Olympic Games were on and Miss Fisher, the Matron by now, lent me a radio. The only problem was that the radio would overheat and from time to time I would have to let it cool down.

I was sorry not to be able to catch-up with John but it was impossible... next time. I have just been looking at my copy of 'Cricketers in the Making' which is the copy that Denys Wilcox sent my father and it has kind words written in it. John is, for the most part, the batsman and I the bowler.

Thank you for taking us to the new premises over Thorpe Bay way and for showing us around. We thoroughly enjoyed meeting some of the children and most particularly talking with your group... responsive, well mannered and pleasantly inquisitive. It was quite clear to me that although the bricks and mortar may be new to the school, that its 'soul' had travelled well and the 'spirit' remains the same. One way and another, Judy and I have spent much of our lives in boarding and we quickly feel the atmosphere within schools. As we drove away from you we both remarked how much we liked the 'feel' within the Alleyn Court Community... natural and happy.

On our way back to South Australia we spent a few days in India. While at Agra we visited the Taj Mahal... it is breathtaking and I had never really known about the love story behind it all and the reason for its being built in the first place. While there I had a thought... Next year, I'm off for a few months again to the Aboriginal School at Marree. It's a small school (about 50 on a good day) very close to the southern shores of Lake Eyre. The children are quite exceptional, they know their Dreaming Stories and Marree is where the Strzelecki, Oodnadatta and Birdsville tracks meet. It was also on the original Ghan Railway Line, Bullocky Road and Overland Telegraph Line. They have computers and I'm sure would love to make contact with Alleyn Court... it could be a most interesting exchange of cultures. William Wilcox might be particularly interested in this idea. I'll be up there between January and July and here until then.

There we are, Richard, I've rambled on a bit and I don't know if from this you can extract anything for next year's celebrations. Have a great year and I would always be grateful to be kept posted.

On reflection it is fun for me to have known five generations of the Wilcox family!

Take care . . . all the best,
Campbell Whalley.

Stephen Bishop who retired as joint headmaster in 2004 after 26 years at A.C.

Paul Green, Joint-Headmaster, to whom fell, with Stephen Bishop and William Wilcox, the onerous task of moving A.C. from its former site to Wakering Road

Richard Chandler who will lead A.C. into its second century as sole Head

William Wilcox, A.C. pupil, teacher, joint-headmaster and parent!

The History Lesson

'Tomorrow', said the Professor of Archaeology, 'we are going to visit the land of our ancestors.' The melodramatic note of this announcement was deliberate, if out of character, and his students responded as anticipated with the stillness of attention.

'A transit ship is booked, and a companion ship also to bring the excavators. We should manage an inspection sufficient to our purpose before nightfall and our return. Please bring your own food for the day. Finally, I have two texts for you to study. As you will see they are short and both written by the same man, a Mathematics Don at the University of Oxford during the nineteenth century. I will explain the connection in a moment.'

He handed them out. On a single sheet two extracts were printed, the first from a diary, the second from a letter:

Tuesday 19th December 1876
Heard of the death of my dear cousin, and friend of thirty years, William Wilcox. I had telegraphed on hearing of his illness, to offer to go and help to nurse him...

Christ Church, Oxford, February 7th, 1877
My dear Fanny,
I have a favour to ask of you. I have taken a liberty which I hope you will forgive of getting Margaret to tell me about your circumstances, that I might offer help towards educating the children. I rejoice to be able to do such a thing for dear Williams's sake. And now will you kindly let me send you £30 a year, paid half-yearly in advance . . . .

With love to the children,
I am ever yours affectionately

C.L. Dodgson.

P.S. Of course I can only promise this during my life, and, if I had heavy losses, I might not be able to continue it. But I see no reason to fear having to withdraw or reduce it.

'Now the site we are to visit and examine', he continued, 'was known as Founder's Hall, and the founder was one of the children educated by Mr Dodgson's kindness. Without the education made possible by his generosity, to found a school would have been impossible. See you tomorrow at 9 o'clock sharp.'

The arrival of the ships was seen, or more accurately foreseen, by another teacher, many, many years before. Being of one blood with both the Professor and founder and as a result of the way he was dealing with this seventh lesson on Friday, the last lesson of the week, the moment found him in a particularly receptive state of mind.

Lewis Carroll

It was 2B for History and though it could not be said for all the class, the teacher had learned a thing or two. They would go to the library - too much of the day was spent in the confines of their classroom.

'Now all of you', said the teacher on their arrival, 'all of you have a chosen historical character about whom you are going to talk or write. I want you to begin a search for information. To begin with it will be in silence and on your own. Take notes as appropriate. After ten minutes or so I'll try and help if you're in difficulties. Any questions?'

'Sir...'

'Yes, John...'

'Why do we learn History, Sir?'

The children's faces turned towards him. After all it was a question with which many felt a sympathy even if few had the wit and nerve to articulate it.

A photograph taken by Lewis Carroll in 1863 of his cousins William and Fanny Wilcox.

They were 'the heartiest of hosts and hostesses'

'That's a good question... a very good question. I would like first to think about it and answer next week. We must discuss it altogether then. But I'll tell you one thing immediately. You've chosen Lewis Carroll haven't you?'

'Yes, Sir.'

'Well if it hadn't been for him you wouldn't be sitting here now. I'll explain that another time but you see we learn from History that actions have consequences. Now I've told you what to do; please get on. I'll be coming round in about ten minutes.'

A somewhat reluctant browsing began. But soon, noting it to be quiet and purposeful the teacher turned to the northern window and looked out over the school below.

Perhaps History was perspective for the consequences of present actions can only be guessed at whilst those of the past can be traced. Anyway he was pondering the boy's question when he saw, in his mind's eye the ships land, and witnessed the activity which followed.

Using an X-Ray photograph of the simple four walled structure the excavators had been programmed to remove the accumulated debris down to the depth of the original floor. A few interesting shapes had also shown up within this area and they were left, but it was not long before the original interior of the Hall was clear and using handbrushes and other tools it was possible to uncover the walls and the evidence they harboured.

Founder's Hall

Their discoveries were not difficult to categorise. Among the gymnasium equipment was the metal-frame of a trampoline with the canvas almost completely rotted away. Traces of vaulting horses, wall-bars, and fencing equipment were also found and identified.

It was probable also that the Hall was used for Assembly for on the West Wall was a metal plaque embossed with a prayer. It took them some time to make out all the words but finally they managed it. 'The Knight's Prayer.' It read:

My Lord God, I am ready on the threshold of this new day to go forth armed with thy power, seeking adventure to right the wrong and overcome evil. In all things to serve thee bravely, faithfully,

**joyfully, that at the end of the day's labour, kneeling for thy bless-
ing, thou mayst find no stain upon my shield.**

Above it had been a circular window. Only traces of the original stained glass
remained but the glass shapes could be made out by the lead which held them.
In the centre had been a cross. There were the remains of a piano also.

They found traces of decaying board fixed to the walls, with the gilt lettering
almost completely obliterated; perhaps Honours' Boards of some description.

Above the main door and in a good state of preservation was a commemora-
tive stone bearing the inscription:

Founder's Hall
In memory of
Theodore Robert Wilcox
Founder and Headmaster of
Alleyn Court Preparatory School
1904-1932

On their journey home there would be a chance to evaluate the evidence.

'What have you learned about these people – our ancestors?' the Professor
would ask his students.

'Well, it was a Christian school and no doubt each day started with an
Assembly,' said one. 'Their's was a gospel of love.'

'And they placed considerable emphasis on physical fitness', said another.

'No doubt the Honours Boards honoured academic achievements, but anyway
we know a school would have to place high value on the academic and the pur-
suit of truth and wisdom', said a third.

'Yes', said the Professor. 'They were Christian and they attached importance
to wisdom and physical fitness. What else do we know about them?'

'They destroyed themselves.'

The students laughed at the incongruity but the old man turned his face away.

'It's not really funny, is it? My family lived and died there. I'm glad we found no bones today... anyway you think about it... particularly about what created and what destroyed...'

'Please, sir, have you a pen I could borrow?'

The teacher looked back to the library again.

'Here you are', and reaching in his jacket pocket he pulled out his marking pen. A card, pulled out in the pen's clasp, dropped to the floor. He handed over the pen and picked up the card which he recognised as something his wife had left for him on the kitchen table the day after her birthday.

He reminded himself of the words written there:

Thank you for the present, darling. Remember the past.
Look forward to the future.

Before he had always thought of tenses as self-contained, so isolated. Although conveniently neat for a teacher of grammar, in the more important world past, present and future were separated by so tiny a fraction of time as to be inseparable, entirely dependent on one another, a continuum still for all the comings and goings of individual lives.

On his way home that day he bought his wife some flowers, lilies of the valley. It was to say thank you for helping him to answer the boy's question.

Lines from **Lent**, Michael Wilcox's 'Alleyn Court play' first performed at the Lyric Studio, Hammersmith, in 1983.

Paul: The boys would all be in bed by now. I sleep with them, rather than in my own room. The place seems so quiet without them, even at this time of night. The classrooms all have their own smell... ink and wood. The changing rooms smell of socks and damp mud. The back lavatories, where we play marbles, of old disinfectant and lavatory paper. If you took me into any part of the school I could tell you exactly where I was just by using my nose. On a night like this, any sound that I hear... the closing of a door... a flush of water... tells me who is where, and what they are doing. I know this whole place. It's where I've spent my entire life. I've been to London three times, but not since my parents died. Since then, I've only been to Newbury, and to some of the nearby schools to play football and cricket. In term time, the Daily Telegraph is put into the library each day. Mr Edwards gives us lectures about not just reading the sports pages. There's no paper at all in the holidays. Mrs Blake never has one. I try to listen to the news on the radio.

There's a sound on the stair.

I can hear Matey coming down to raid the kitchen. He's been doing this since before I was born!

Paul: In the dormitory, mine's the only bed with a mattress on. I mean in the holidays. On the last morning of term, all the boys carry their mattresses into Ruskin dorm . . . it's above the boiler room. All the other beds in my dorm look like black skeletons at night time! I stubbed my toe on one in the middle of last night. Sometimes I wake up and wonder why it's so quiet. Then in the mornings I lie there in a doze, waiting for Matey to come round with the bell. He makes a terrific noise! He doesn't do it in the holidays, of course. On the last morning of term, we all throw things at him... like wet flannels and slippers! It's all terrific fun! There's still two weeks left of the holidays, then the boys' trunks start to turn up, and matron and the domestic staff come back and everything gets cleaned, and the masters turn up. There's a new master next term. There nearly always is.

It's quite embarassing not being a prefect, even in your last term. Everyone will ask why, and think I've done something wrong. You can't keep explaining that the headmaster is a rotten worm.

At least there's cricket and Music Club and the best ever puppet show. And Matthew Dolan. He's my friend. There's quite a lot to look forward to...

The closing bars of the Elgar concerto...